personal
space

creating a home that expresses your individuality

personal
space

kate worsley

conran

To John

First published in 2000 by
Conran Octopus Limited
a part of Octopus Publishing Group
2-4 Heron Quays
London E14 4JP

www.conran-octopus.co.uk

Commissioning Editor: Catriona Woodburn
Assistant Editor: Lucy Nicholson
Copy Editor: Galiena Hitchman
Art Editor: Sue Storey
Picture Researcher: Clare Limpus
Proofreaders: Barbara Roby, Colette Campbell
Indexer: Hilary Bird
Production Controllers: Sarah Tucker, Alex Wiltshire

British Library Cataloguing-in-Publication Data. A catalogue
record for this book is available from the British Library.

ISBN 1-84091-126-3

Printed in China

contents

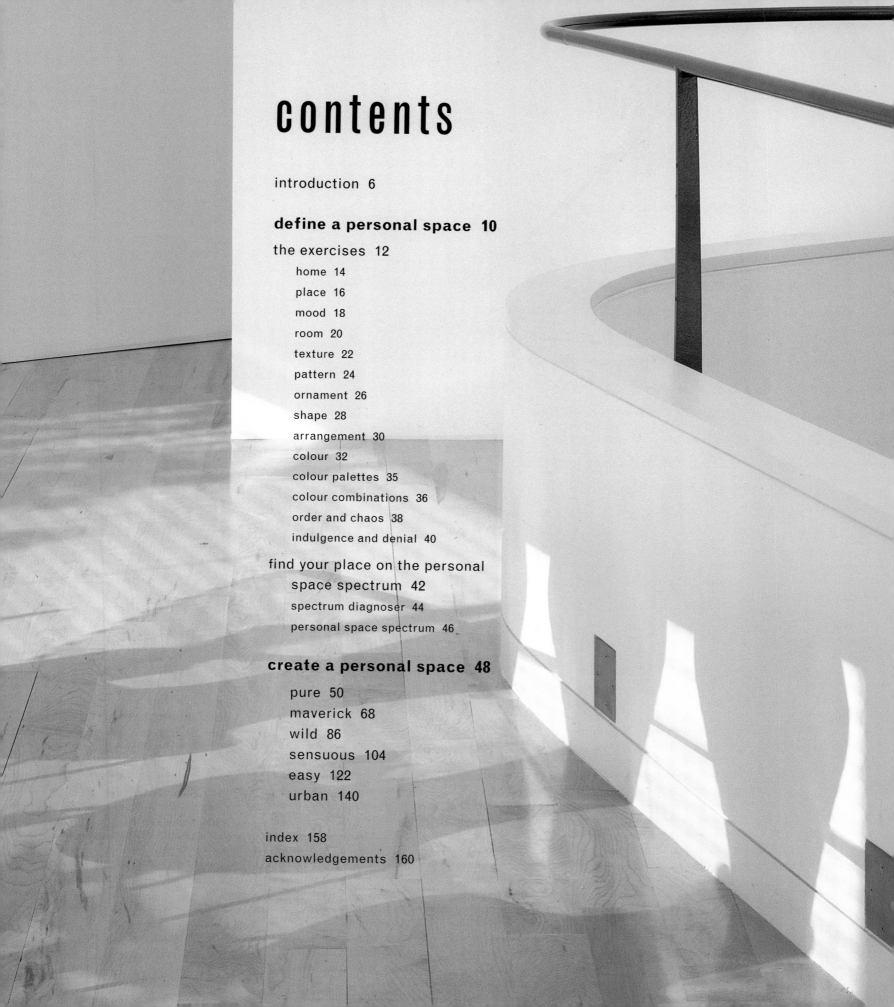

introduction

This is a book about interior decoration which is as much about the interior of your mind as it is about the interior of your home. Of course it deals with objects and colour, and style and mood. But it views them in the reflected light of the only factor that ultimately gives them any value: your personality. When it comes to decorating your home, exploring and defining how you feel about these things is what matters most. If you are to be happy in your own home, whatever you introduce into it must first satisfy your inner needs, not some received notion of style or acceptability.

A home is a personal space, to do with as we wish. Any sort of public space – office, bar, restaurant, railway station – has to play to the crowd, make a style statement in order to stand out. Your home is the arena in which your intimate life is played out, at its own pace and in its own way. It doesn't have to speak to anyone else but you.

A public place is usually designed to meet pressing practical needs, and indeed a personal space can be equally utilitarian. Alternatively we can print our personality on it, infuse it with our own spirit. A house is like a garden: left barren it will give little back; nurtured and cherished it will provide comfort, sustenance and inspiration. You will feel the benefit, and anyone visiting you will feel it, too.

If a home has character it is immediately obvious. It adds up to more than the sum of its parts. Unlike an interior professionally designed for a glossy magazine

or a television makeover, a characterful home is not designed to sell you something, it simply gives you something. Interiors magazines often pore over homes that are the compelling creation of a particularly vivid personality. Then they isolate elements that can be replicated easily in your own home: a paint finish, or a certain style of table. Curiously, however, as a sort of shorthand for style, these individual items often work far less well out of context. That elusive quality, personal style, fails to translate. It is the one thing you can't buy.

But you can develop it. And once you develop it, once you learn to trust your own taste, you can blend those individual items gleaned from all over the place into a home that is truly yours. This book is about how you can develop the ability to hold the style of your home together by the force of your personality, not by slavishly copying the effects achieved by others. It hopes to inspire you to be yourself, and to be inspired to create your own personal space.

Over our lifetimes, numerous factors influence how we would like our homes to be. Understanding and making the most of these influences is what this book is all about. These influences are as individual as DNA, and should be respected. They provide a blueprint for a personal style that no one else can hijack and call theirs.

Conversely, if you model your personal space on someone else's, you are betraying your own history. Try to liberate yourself from the tyranny of fashion, which now influences interiors more than ever before. The turnover of desirable styles and approaches has speeded up to match the level of seasonal changes in clothing. Watch any television makeover programme and you might see mauve infiltrating bedrooms in the spring, and another colour taking over six months later.

While there are far more things to buy for the home now, and at lower prices, the range of styles and colours available at any one time is increasingly determined and limited by commercial trends.

These interiors trends are the antithesis of personal style. We all know people who only a couple of years ago enthusiastically decorated in the most up-to-the-minute style they could concoct from what was on offer in shops and magazines. Now, of course, thanks to the influence of those same magazines and stores, their home looks dated, and they're tiring of it already. It is fashion's old trap: everyone thinks they're leading when they're following.

Before fashion, of course, the issue of respectability and 'good taste' was the major external influence on how you decorated your home. When capitalism first made taste an issue for the masses, people turned to interiors manuals to discover what was acceptable in polite society. Author Edith Wharton, in her incarnation as society decorator, urged a return to Italianate architectural principles of rhythm and logic as the antidote to what she called the 'superficial application of ornament' and 'dubious eclecticism' introduced since 1800. By the twentieth century, coordinating the colours of walls with ceilings, floors and furnishings had become a central preoccupation. All sorts of rules emerged, which look risible in retrospect. Many older people still hold that certain colours should not be seen together in the same room, or even used in decoration at all.

Now, of course, we are all individuals, and want our homes to reflect the fact. But if we let ourselves want only what everyone else wants, and at the same time, then our homes will reflect back to us every commercial cliché going, not our own taste at all. 'Taste is the only morality,' wrote the critic and writer

John Ruskin. 'Tell me what you like, and I'll tell you who you are. A thing is worth precisely what it can do for you, not what you choose to pay for it.'

What if our couple with the démodé home had really thought about what they wanted their home to be before they turned to the shops and magazines for inspiration? What if they had asked themselves not just about which colours worked in which rooms, or which sofas looked 'cool', but what were, for them, the elements that make a home feel like home?

The parallel with fashionable clothes works here, too. Most of us are looking for a style of clothing that suits our personality, lifestyle and body type. But if you get it wrong along the way, filling your wardrobe with expensive mistakes is one thing, living with a household of junk is another. Edith Wharton also wrote: 'It seems easier to most people to arrange a room like someone else's than to analyse and express their own needs.' This is still true. Her belief that men are less slaves to 'the feminine tendency to want things because other people have them, rather than to have things because they are wanted', may seem rather dated, however.

Buying on impulse is rarely successful, unless you really know what works for you. Why buy a traditional two-seater sofa with high arms because it suits the period in which your home was built, only to end up hating its compact proportions because you like to lie down to watch television? Or strip the floorboards because it looks up to date, when you prefer to walk around barefoot all day? Only if doing this fulfils some other, more complicated need in you, will it make any sense.

It is in our nature to invest much in material objects that transcend the purely practical. The most mundane object can function as talisman, touchstone, souvenir or emblem. When institutions such as the army, prisons or the church want to deny their members privileges, or concentrate their minds on communal matters, a tried-and-tested technique is to remove personal effects from rooms.

Now, however, thanks partly to the pressure to keep selling us new things, we have come to set more store by how things look – and, increasingly, how they feel – rather than by what they mean to us. Since the implications of mass production sank in, companies have been trying to 'design in' personality, meaning and emotional attachment to domestic objects. And, of course, we respond to this increasingly subtle language of persuasion, but only up to a point.

Recently, the quality-of-life index in Britain was expanded from simply recording access to consumer goods to include intangibles such as pollution and congestion. More and more people are realizing that the quality of the home is also determined by things that cannot be bought. There is value in having somewhere to sit by the window as the sun sets, a view of the garden from your bed, or a stool that reminds you of your grandfather, for instance. Or even keeping about you a particular colour or material that means a lot, for whatever reason.

As American writer Akiko Busch expresses it in Geography of Home, 'The more we personalize our possessions, the more we are able to see ourselves in them. And once we have invested ourselves in the things we own, it is difficult to be rid of them. Which is why I am certain that sentimentality is grossly undervalued as one of our most important and genuine emotions. For what is sentimentality after all but... a way of attaching worth to personal history with a sense of lightness, rather than with inevitable and potent psychological meaning?'

Talking about having an emotional relationship with your furniture may seem alarmingly unhinged. After all, as a joke from the 1980s had it, designers are people who treat objects like women. I'm not suggesting that the process of personalizing your space should take precedence over your human relationships, but that you acknowledge the emotional dimension of the objects that make up your home, and that you make your human relationships and your attitude to them an integral part of how you approach them.

Your home environment supports your identity, as do your activities, although whether these three elements are in tune depends on how truthful you are with yourself. If you find yourself lavishing extraordinary amounts of care and attention on your home, or creating a home environment that is very different from that which you inhabit in the outside world, examine your lifestyle carefully. Filling your home with the trappings of a stylish house will not, in the long run, do anything to sustain a lonely or unfulfilled heart. But you can create a home that brings out the best in you, that helps you to function as you ought.

Your personal space mirrors your loves and dreams just as much as it reflects your life. This book helps you to explore all three, and shows how the ways of living that they suggest can be incorporated into your home. Most of us depend on places to provide an external framework that helps us structure our inner lives and bring about 'flow', the term coined by psychologist Mihaly Csikszentmihalyi to describe that satisfactory sense of being in the midst of life. *Personal Space* is intended to help you create just such a place.

define a personal space

Every room in our home echoes who we are, and reveals something about the influences and experiences that have shaped us. Some of the choices we make in the home are conscious and deliberate, others are prompted by motives we barely understand. The more we know about what we instinctively want in the home, the clearer we can be about what we are trying to achieve and the easier it will be to create an environment in which we feel at home.

The exercises that follow look at ideals, furnishings, colour and lifestyle, and enable you to examine your instinctive responses and conscious choices. They will help you to understand your motives and so set your own goals.

the exercises

How and where we grew up, what we saw and experienced along the way, and how we aspire to lead our lives in the future – all these things feed into what sort of home we make for ourselves, as well as how we dream it could be better.

These exercises cover the four major areas in which we apply personal style: the ideals we hold, the furnishings we prefer, the colours we like and the lifestyle we maintain. Working through these areas, the exercises will help you to understand your initial reactions, explore your intuition, and identify unexplored themes. Your responses will then help you to find your place on the Personal Space Spectrum (see pages 46–47), a graphic depiction of attitudes to the home which allows you to visualize how the values that are fundamental to a whole range of sensibilities contrast and overlap. This spectrum is your guide to the second part of the book, which deals with how to create a personal space.

How to approach the exercises

Firstly, you will be asked to explore your dreams and aspirations. What is most important to you about a house – from its physical environment, to its emotional and cultural atmosphere, to the room you prefer to spend most time in? Next, you should consider your material preferences. What textures, shapes and arrangements are most pleasing to your eye or touch? What makes a particular lamp or cushion, for instance, 'jump out' at you in a shop? Then, think about how you react to colours. Which colours mean most to you? What colour combinations do you like and dislike? Finally, don't overlook how you use your home, on a day-to-day basis. How organized are you? How much do you like to indulge your senses? How receptive does your home have to be to social gatherings, or children, or work?

Each exercise can be approached on two levels. The simplest way is to provide a brief response in the form of key words. Sample key words are provided with each exercise. This is not a test, so if you find you cannot decide between two responses, just choose both. You can use the suggested key words or write down your own as they occur to you. Then turn to page 42 for guidance on how the key words let you find your place on the Personal Space Spectrum.

The other method is to use the questions raised by the exercises to explore your own sensibility further, adding and analysing more background detail. This demands more effort, but can be immensely rewarding. You will build up a clearer idea of your potential personal space and have a lot more material to help you find your place on the Personal Space Spectrum.

After asking you for your key words, each exercise invites you to think further about your responses. Write down your thoughts, in note form if you like, make sketches, and add any other material that comes to mind. Using a ring binder or large notebook allows you to add pages or leave space for later notes and ideas. Do this, and you are on your way to creating your own personal space file, a record of what is most important to you in a home and how to achieve it.

If you can, think about the exercises over a few days. A quiet weekend at home is ideal. If you find it hard to focus, use magazines, old and new, for inspiration. Choosing some that you would otherwise not normally look at can help clarify your responses. Flick through them as you work through the exercises, cutting out images and items that illustrate your thoughts. You can attach these to the relevant pages of your personal space file.

Carry on adding thoughts and images to your notes for as long as you like, updating and modifying your responses as you get to know yourself better. You may face a dramatic upheaval in your life – perhaps you will move a great distance, or the people who make up your household will change. It can be a good idea to start a new set of notes at times like these. Our ideas about how we like to live can change enormously over a lifetime. If, in the future, you work through the exercises again you may find your responses differ. Very often, however, despite a radical change in circumstances, you will discover a thread of continuity, or even that you have come back to where you started.

home

Each time we create a new home for ourselves we are driven by the echoes of previous homes and our vision of what a real home could be. Consciously or not, we try to realize a particular set of ideals. And as George Sand wrote, people either dream of living in a palace or in a cottage.

Ranch house out of the way, ramshackle, freethinking

Château grand, lavish, fairy tale

Penthouse cool, funky, streamlined

Cottage pretty, nostalgic, peaceful

Tropical beach hut exotic, luscious, close to nature

Tower original, ambitious, conceptual

Perversely, the yearning for simplicity is likely to be greater when we are living well, and vice versa. French poet Saint-Pol-Roux retreated to a simple Brittany fisherman's cottage, but before long he had built a manor house around it – a palace with eight towers.

Dream homes are also about safety and adventure. Childhood homes, whether accurately remembered or fantasy, are a place of refuge in our minds and form a blueprint for living to which we cannot help but adhere.

At the same time we construct an ideal home, where all our hopes for the future reside. As the place we are moving towards, it constantly undergoes renovation and improvement. Psychoanalyst Carl Jung famously built himself a house at Bollingen on Lake Zürich, gradually adding towers, courtyard and loggia, as the external manifestations of his psyche.

Imagining your dream home

Look at the homes pictured below and imagine what it would be like to live in each one. Which of them exerts the greatest pull on your imagination? When you are fed up with your own home, what sort of building do you wish you could live in? With all the money and opportunity in the world, what sort of home would you buy or build for yourself? From the homes pictured, choose the one that comes closest to your own dream home.

Now think of up to three key words to describe what attracts you to the home you have chosen, or use the sample words appearing alongside the captions on the left-hand page. Write down your choice, along with your key words. (If you are drawn to two homes equally, then include both.)

You may also have a specific dream home in mind that none of the pictures approximates to. Write this down too, along with the words to describe it. If you cannot get a clear picture, consider houses that you have visited or images that you have seen and felt drawn to. These could be homes you lived in as a child, or somewhere you stayed while on holiday. Maybe it's a Mediterranean villa, a teepee, a Georgian town house, an eco-lodge, dacha, yacht, Moorish palace, log cabin, Gothic folly or even a monastery.

You should now have an idea of what elements are most important to you in a home. Look objectively at your current home. Does it have any of the qualities of your dream home? What are they? And what is missing? Note down the qualities and features that come to mind. These will be explored in later exercises.

A useful exercise is to visualize your ideal home. Shut your eyes and see what it looks like from the outside. How many levels is it on? What style is it built in? Where is the front door? When you enter, what is the first thing that you see? Which are the first rooms that you go into? What are they like? Explore in your mind, noting elements and atmosphere. Think of three key words to describe it.

place

Where a home is set can evoke a much more powerful response than the home itself. When we see a hut clinging to a windswept mountainside, a cabin alone on an open plain, or a farm nestled in a green valley, it can feel as though the geography of such places could contain our state of mind like a hand in a glove. If we cannot always go to those places that have most meaning for us, then we can at least bring something of their message indoors.

It is possible to regulate psychology with geography, as American journalist Winifred Gallagher realized after she bought a house in the woods of upstate New York, simply because it felt like home, and provided the perfect antidote to her stressful city life. In her book *The Power of Place*, she proposes that people who are sluggish and delicate respond to homes that open easily to the elements – wide open windows and long views. The hypersensitive and allergic gravitate to static, enclosed spaces, where the air is still and the temperature consistent: courtyards not hillsides. Being able to observe easily from your home any agitated

Lagoon intense, colourful, vivid

City energizing, powerful, hectic

Market varied, bustling, amusing

Lake serene, harmonious, gentle

Virgin forest profuse, all-enveloping, heated

Foreshore elemental, bracing, clean

feature of the landscape – a marketplace, a waterfall, a main road – provides a sustaining sense of being part of a larger scheme, if that is what you feel you need.

The Romantic movement gave us a vision of the wild places of the world as havens, not as sites of fear and reverence. 'I live not in myself, but I become/ Portion of that around me; and to me/High mountains are a feeling, but the hum/Of human cities torture' wrote Byron in *Childe Harold's Pilgrimage*. Later, Welsh poet Dylan Thomas found that the wildness of the Boat House at Laugharne, his 'sea-shaken house/on a breakneck of rock', matched his own wildness. And in her elegy to motherhood, *The Blue Jay Sings*, Louise Erdrich praises the aptness of her self-sufficient little house in an area of fecund countryside.

Imagining your dream environment

From the places pictured, choose the environment you find most congenial and note up to three key words to describe what makes it attractive to you. What other settings would you love for your ideal home? Deep inside the woods? Surrounded by meadows of grazing horses? Now think of the landscapes you find particularly moving. Do you know what it is that you love about them? If mountains thrill you, is it because they make you feel small, or powerful, or detached? Do deserts make you feel purified or lost? Write down the three words that sum up the emotions evoked by your favourite places.

You should now have an idea of what is most important to you about your physical environment. Perhaps a view is not as important to you as the lie of the land, the climate, or the density of population. Your physical constitution may affect how you feel about this more than you might expect.

mood

Mood is like odour, it will pervade a room before it can be traced to its source. But you usually recognize it as soon as you enter. At some point in our lives, most of us find that the mood – the culture and atmosphere – of a particular time or place come to mean a lot to us for whatever reason. We immerse ourselves in books and films relating to our interest, or surround ourselves with items that emit some of its essence.

The minute you step into a holiday cottage you may feel a sense of *déjà vu* because in many small ways it reminds you of your grandfather's house – something to do with the steepness of the staircase and the way the windows open and the colour of the upholstery. Then you may realize that houses of that era always excite you. Any mention of that period in books and magazines seems to leap out at you, you find yourself drawn to furniture in shops that seems somehow familiar. Very often re-creating such an atmosphere becomes the unspoken goal of your homemaking.

Even when you find yourself drawn to a particular period in time or a place that you have never

Morocco loose, informal, relaxed

Art Deco sharp, impressive, glamorous

Zen meditative, impassive, freeing

Mogul heady, languorous, rhapsodic

Shaker ordered, unpretentious, well-crafted

Gothic florid, vulgar, mad

experienced – the world of the early American settlers, or life in a Russian city during a long winter – the feeling can be just as intense.

Imagining an ideal mood

Look at the pictures of rooms from different countries and historical periods and choose the culture with which you feel most affinity. You may find the fabled life of Indian emperors immensely attractive and slip into a reverie just looking at the image on the page. Or perhaps you simply enjoy the bracing spiritual order and practicality of the nineteenth-century Shaker communities. Is there another mood that captivates you? When and where would you like to have lived and why? Do you enjoy Egyptian art? Does the hand-to-mouth life of a Scottish crofter answer a need in you to pit yourself against the elements? Write down your choice, and up to three key words that describe the atmosphere with which you feel most kinship.

Creating your ideal mood

I'm not suggesting that you literally decorate your home as if it were an Egyptian palace, or log cabin or Indian shrine (although many people are happy to do just that). Rather, you should think about what the culture means to you in terms of its style and its values. The pace of life, the way interiors were illuminated, and the importance of food and nature, religion and hierarchy. What does it remind you of, or make you wish you had? Adventure, romance, security, novelty and authenticity are all common cravings. Of course, you could simply like Egyptian turquoise or Easter Island statues on a material level. But a cultural fondness that is hard to dislodge can be well rooted in some deeper meaning.

room

Almost every room, every space in a home is loaded with meaning: the cellar filled with foreboding; the kitchen that renews itself daily as the living, breathing hub of the household; the parlour that presents an acceptable façade to disguise a home in turmoil; the bathroom as sanctuary or isolation cell; the bedroom overflowing with associations from birth through sex and to death. As for the attic, the tower and the room with a view, they can be whatever you want them to be.

American psychologist Mihaly Csikszentmihalyi believes that men and women prefer different areas of the house. 'Men often consider the basement to be the best bit of the house, while women favour the bathroom. To a man, the basement is a retreat, a place for hobbies, a workshop, a bar, or a game room, but to a woman it means loading the washing machine or a problem with the boiler. In the bathroom, surrounded by the accoutrements that help her establish her identity, she feels safe. And while the kitchen is usually more important to women, it represents obligation as well as pleasure to them.'

Identifying your favourite room

Which room in a house is most important to you? When you come home, where do you seek sanctuary? Do you feel drawn to ground level, or do you want to rise above everything, drawing up the ladder behind you? Perhaps you see yourself as a sentinel and like to be near the entrance. Or do you like the household to circulate around you, and gravitate to the main living area? What room does your home lack?

From these pictures, choose the room in which you would feel most comfortable. Try to focus on the room and its uses and meaning rather than the style of the decor. Write down your choice and use up to three key words to describe it. Consider other rooms. Would you love a garden room? A turret room?

In which rooms do you spend as little time as possible? The bathroom, perhaps, because washing is a bore, or the bedroom, because you want to get on with living rather than lying around. Which room could you do without, or merge with another? A library-cum-kitchen, for instance? Think, too, about what elements in a room are important to you. Would a simple, structurally unfussy box with as few angles and features as possible satisfy you?

Living room sophisticated, sociable, fine living

Kitchen hard-working, nurturing, ergonomic

Bathroom clean, separate, secure

Study stimulating, bolstering, fun

Dining room indulgent, greedy, extravagant

Bedroom cosseting, welcoming, dreamy

texture

Texture is a powerful tool in making your home your own. Novel textures stimulate, while the familiar soothe. When visiting someone else's home, you may find that turning their doorknob, lifting their kettle, or settling down on their sofa actually feels strange; because the textures of their life differ from yours. But spend enough time in any home, and you will become accustomed to it. And in your own home, with objects you have chosen, the process of familiarization is even more subliminal. The texture of the armchair you bought so long ago has become so familiar you can recognize it in the dark: you reach out for it as a staging post on the way to turning on the light.

You can use this process to help make your home a more comforting place to be. Choose textures that answer something in you and let them become part of the fabric of your life; just as a signature scent which comes to seem less noticeable to the wearer, yet still announces its presence to others.

Concrete industrial, strong, solid

Wool natural, traditional, warm

Old paint unpredictable, sense of history, haphazard

Leather animal warmth, smells good, sexy

Perspex modern, clear, adaptable

Feathers frivolous, light, delicate

Considering materials and textures

Look at the materials in these six pictures. Ignore the objects and their colour, and focus on the basic qualities of the materials. Do not let yourself be put off if, for example, you prefer leather to be smooth, not buttoned as here, or Perspex when it is coloured. Perhaps your first reaction is that some of these materials are old-fashioned or even trendy clichés. Put these thoughts aside. Simply imagine touching each one and decide which you would most enjoy in your home. Record your choices and up to three qualities that explain why they appeal to you.

Now consider other textures, which do not appear here, that you strongly like or dislike. What feelings, associations and memories do they evoke for you? Establish in your own mind which textures give you a shiver of delight, and which positively repel you. Make notes about these.

Applying your thinking to your home

Your goal is to create a home full of textures to which you respond on first contact, and then which make you feel good as you live with them. You will want to combine textures that stimulate and soothe to the degree that suits you. If you think of your home as a sanctuary, which textures signify security and fastness to you? Do you find acres of burnished steel reassuringly durable or off-puttingly clinical? Can you bear extreme contrasts, or absence, of texture in your home? Be honest with yourself. You may think of yourself as a 'sensuous being,' when other factors, such as how easy something is to clean, may play a larger part in your choice of textures than you like to admit. Now look around you. How much of your chosen textures do you currently have in your home?

pattern

This is one area where most people can say what they don't like far more readily than what they do. There are so many patterns, and so many places to use them, it's hardly surprising when people avoid the issue and opt for plain materials instead. Because a pattern can be so rich in information, deciding on one you like can be far more complicated than choosing a colour. But finding fabrics, tiles and wallpapers you can live with is easier if you know what you are reacting to in a pattern.

Understanding patterns

Think about how stimulating to the eye, or 'busy', you like patterned surfaces to be. Look around you, and see what your eye is drawn to. Everyday sights – items on shelves, branches outside the window, cars in the car park, diminishing perspectives, clouds in the sky, road maps and smashed glass – all may have elements you respond to. Do you tend to prefer randomness to regularity, curves to angles, density to sparseness? Do you find it soothing to trace the lines of a paisley pattern, or prefer the challenge of finding the order in a seeming jumble of shapes? Is the subtlety of abstract forms stimulating or dull? Do you love to see patterns mixed up together, as in some patchworks, or would an isolated dose of rich pattern in a sea of plainness be enough for you?

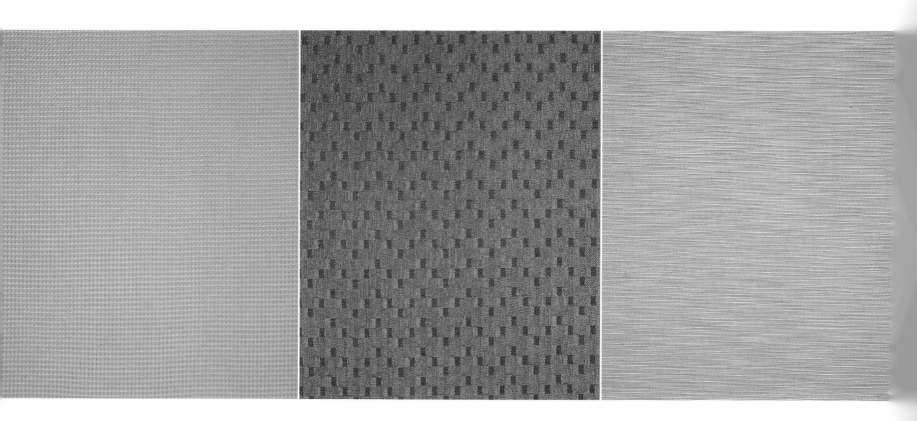

Finding patterns you like

The six different patterns shown here range from the understated to the ornate. Choose the one you would most like to have in your home, even if in only a small quantity. Try to ignore the colourways and concentrate on the contrasts of form and lines. Remember that although one pattern may attract your attention initially, you may not enjoy living with it long-term. Note your choice, along with up to three key words to describe why you like it.

Perhaps your favourite sort of pattern is not here. Do you have one in particular? What associations does it have for you? If you like pop art patterns, for instance, is it because you remember the Swinging Sixties, or because you wish you did?

Geometric regular, restrained, minimal

Tessellate lush, intricate, lulling

Weave quiet, unadulterated, basic

Stripe unaffected, straightforward, easy

Curlicue whimsical, jolly, mind-boggling

Damask wild, over the top, regal

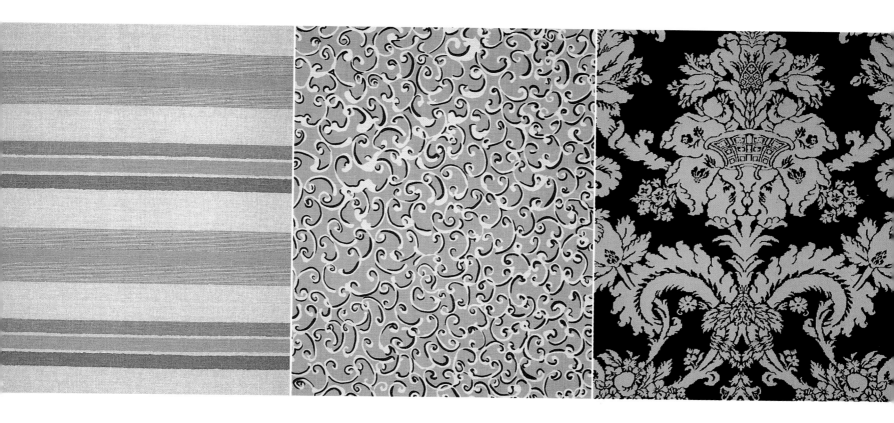

ornament

Ornament can be just as annoying as pattern if you get it wrong, and just as satisfying if you get it right. Your preferences for patterned surfaces and ornamented objects are likely to overlap to some degree: people usually feel comfortable with a similar degree of embellishment in both. How much messing about with basic forms such as chair legs, picture frames and mouldings can you take?

Understanding ornamentation

The degree of ornament we apply to household objects has always had implications beyond the purely aesthetic. For some people, ornamentation is a matter of guilt versus indulgence, opposing the elements of desire and necessity: from the Puritan drive to purge the Christian church of false idols and devilish distractions, to the Islamic prohibition on depictions of natural forms, and the machine-age imperative for form to follow function. Set against this is the aesthete's hunger for beauty and elaboration, and the innate human impulse to doodle, adorn and embellish. What are the motives behind your choices?

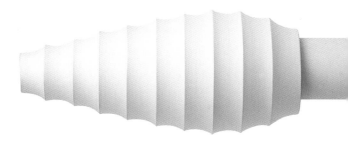

Ribbed unobtrusive, moderate, efficient

Fluted delicate, exquisite, refined

Bundled original, cheap, irregular

Finding your level of ornamentation

These curtain-pole finials all fulfil the same function – keeping the curtain on the pole – but which sort of ornamentation pleases you the most? Make a note of your choice and up to three qualities that you find attractive about it. If you have chosen the wooden globes, for instance, is because you like the smooth, rounded, handcrafted look?

Think about how fussy or plain you like the objects in your home to be. Is your eye pleased by extraneous curves, details, allusions and embellishment, or are you always wishing things could be plainer? Look at the frames you've chosen for your photographs and the stems of your wine glasses. How ornate are they? Do you look at a fringed lampshade and want to rip off the braid, or add more? Is your urge to add – trimmings, bands of decoration, edging, stencils, embroidery – or to subtract? Is there a particular style of ornamentation you love? Do you like your forms primitive or elegant, simple or elaborate?

You may admire a certain austerity or elaborateness in others' homes, but what feels most in tune with your character? You should feel no pressure to be in tune with the times. Just because merchandise in the high street has been coordinated, themed and sold as a package, you don't have to feel that any ornamentation you might like to add – or subtract – would spoil things. What matters is your taste, not the *zeitgeist*.

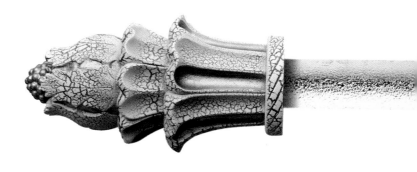

Teardrop attenuated, curved, fine
Balled real, undisguised, traditional
Carved elaborate, classical, complex

shape

After you have absorbed the colours and patterns of a room, the basic forms reveal themselves. Regardless of the material used, characteristic shapes will recur. In some homes, the furniture is solid but not angular, all rectangles with rounded-off corners. In others, you will see a preponderance of spindly, elongated triangular forms, or voluptuously curved solids.

Understanding shapes

The shape of the tables and chairs a person chooses to live with reflects something of their self-image, just as their choice of pet can do. A large, solid person is likely to feel uncomfortable around spindly furniture; although its very delicacy may appeal to someone who yearns to be fragile themselves. Do you want your home to reflect an unpretentious attitude, and fill it with solid durable items? Are primitive shapes inelegant or powerful? Do you see yourself as stable, industrious, quirky, fun, esoteric? Comparing the contours of your silhouette and your self-image with those of your furniture can be quite revealing.

Finding shapes you like

Look at these chairs as shapes only, and forget about how comfortable or fashionable you think they may be. Which pleases you most? Write down your choice and up to three key words that explain its appeal. Now look around you at the major pieces of furniture in your home: the bed, the tables, the seating. Can you see any similarities between their proportions? Wide, low and heavy, perhaps, or upright and finely turned? Do their legs, corners and feet share similar formations? Which pieces are your favourites? Describe their shapes. Which pieces of furniture seem to jar or stand out? Are they very different in shape to the rest?

Fluid integrated, elemental, spare

Angular crisp, clean, proper

Monumental stirring, primitive, grand

Spiral bizarre, inventive, refreshing

Curve smooth, billowing, inviting

Planes scientific, abstract, challenging

arrangement

Imagine an empty surface such as a mantelpiece, shelf or table top. Then think about how many things you could arrange upon it before it stopped feeling empty and started feeling 'full'. Then think about what objects you might put on it and how you might arrange those objects. Unless you are striving for a particular look, how you go about this task is usually unconscious. Whether you choose to display just one object, or a profusion, says something about how dramatic, or impressive or even sentimental you like to be.

Profusion impressive, rich, stimulating

Harmony balanced, expressive, thoughtful

Clusters informal, artless, casual

Asymmetry contemplative, striking, demanding

Clutter themed, intricate, memorabilia

Regularity ordered, complete, severe

Understanding arrangements

Until relatively recently, respectable taste demanded that objects be displayed 'properly', in other words, all lined up symmetrically, each one in its own pool of space, in diminishing order of size or height. So the clock goes in the middle, with a candlestick on either side. The fashion for all things Eastern made sparser, more asymmetrical arrangements popular. But the urge to place something 'off-centre', to break up uniformity, is quite instinctive in some people. Others feel that the simplest possible display enhances rather than detracts from the impact of the object.

Finding arrangements that you like

Look at how you arrange flowers in a vase, or place cushions on a sofa, or set a table. Do you choose a range of shapes and sizes, clustered at random? Do you ensure that two carefully matched and proportioned items are aligned to balance? What effect do you tend to try to achieve? Simple elegance, unexpected juxtaposition, cosy profusion, drama?

Now, looking at the pictures, say which of these six mantelpiece arrangements you prefer. Which grouping most resembles how you would like to arrange the objects in your home? Write down your choice and describe what you like about the effect it achieves using up to three key words.

colour

Colour and light instantaneously affect how we feel and can alter the mood of a room like nothing else. While colour theories and fashions come and go, your own colour repertoire – the various hues that appeal to you – remains unique. Theorists from Aristotle to Goethe, Itten to Panton, have attempted to define and explain colour and how it affects us. No one, as yet, has come up with a definitive answer. All we can know for certain is our own individual response to colour.

Understanding colour

We understand something of colour perception, how the brain responds to different wavelengths; that the eye requires most adjustment to look at red and none at all for green, making these colours respectively the most wearing and most restful. But beyond that is mostly theorizing.

The number of primary colours (from which all other colours can be derived) varies according to who you talk to. Colourists recognize three primary pigments: yellow, blue and red; physicists also use three primary colours, but when mixing light, as in television, these are red, blue and green. Some think black and white do not count as colours, let alone primaries; for others they are essential to produce the full range of colour. Even talking about colour is problematic. A 1960s study found that all languages had a maximum of only 11 terms for colour, yet now, computer graphics have made available millions of colours, far more than the human eye can recognize, let alone name.

The painter Johannes Itten, who taught colour theory at the Bauhaus school in Germany after the First World War, explored the concept of personal aura, the idea that a person has a fundamental set of characteristic colours that mirror their personality, aptitudes and interests. In other words, a painter who likes to use blue, grey and yellow would find working with concrete and glass rewarding. A woman who habitually chose pure, seething colours shot with black would have a lively and concentrated personality, with intense feeling. And an interior decorator whose personal spectrum was dominated by blue-grey would attract clients who were 'chromatically related', while those who were attuned to green or orange would find his interiors uncongenial.

In 1928 Itten assigned his art class various harmonic colour combinations to work with. When, after 20 minutes or so the students became restless, saying that they found his combinations positively discordant and unpleasant, he told them to paint whatever combinations they found harmonious instead. After an hour, each student had produced several sets of harmonious colours of their own. But every student's set of (remarkably similar) combinations was still very different from the others. Itten dubbed this phenomenon 'subjective colour'.

It seems subjective colour is the only sort of colour we can make much sense of. British colour psychologist Angela Wright, who advises companies

Right The twentieth-century Danish designer Verner Panton devised a system of 12 colours that could not clash however they were used together, and a series of rooms (his own home included) to exploit the psychological impact of colour.

on what colours to use in offices and shops, has developed this idea. With colour there are no absolutes, no good or bad colours, only relative perceptions. While people may say that they have their favourite colours, or hues, more important is their preferred variation of it. Someone may say they love green, when actually it is only warm, yellowy greens they like, and they will react against cooler blue-greens.

Wright has linked personality types to seasonal colours. Outgoing and gregarious, but not particularly deep, personalities are drawn to the warm, light and vivid colours of spring. Reserved, intelligent and observant types react well to hazy, bleached-out summer tones. Questioning, fiery and intense autumnal personalities are supported by blazing, rich hues, while detached perfectionists, with natural authority, find anything but the cool tones of winter hard to tolerate. So the various shades, tones and tints of yellow – the spring yellow of daffodils, the autumn yellow of chrysanthemums and cold lemon yellow – will all have their admirers.

Often our preferred colours are those that recall a specific place or memory: the petrol-blue of your father's work shirt, for instance, or the indeterminate gravelly sand of the edge of the desert.

Right German writer Goethe developed and tested Aristotle's colour theories, and put them into practice in his own home in Weimar where he painted different rooms different colours to gauge the mood they created. Unwelcome guests were shown into the green drawing room to dissuade them from lingering.

colour palettes

Finding your colour palette

What sort of colours attract you? These four sets of colours cover a range of colour 'temperatures'; which do you find most agreeable? Write down the name of the set that appeals to you most.

Look at the colours around you. Which do you tend to use for furnishings, and which for clothing? Is there a difference? Remember that your personality and physical colouring is thought to determine the range of colours, and even the variation of those colours, that suits you and brings out the best in you.

Think about intensity of colour. Do you prefer intense, jewel-bright colours, or muted, chalky shades? If you feel uncomfortable with too much colour, you will probably prefer hues that are mixed with black (dulled colours) or with white (pastel colours).

The quality and amount of light you feel a home needs will affect your colour sense, too. Some people cannot bear natural light to be 'polluted' by colour, and want to keep the home in a neutral register. For others, the amount of daylight is less important than the intensity of the visual stimulation.

As you mature, the amount of colour you can take in the home can change, your taste becoming more subtle or bolder. The specific colours you are drawn to may change, but the sorts of combinations you like remain constant: for example, you used to love bright blue and green, now you prefer bright green and yellow.

Try not to be influenced by external colour rules: what colours are fashionable this year, or what you think you should use in certain conditions. Perhaps you feel that where you live should dictate the colours you use. But again, this tells you something about how much you wish to impose yourself on your environment and how important harmony with your surroundings is to you.

Vibrant

Fresh

Calm

Warm

colour combinations

Understanding colour combinations

Where the previous exercise looked at individual colours, this exercise helps you to think about how you like to combine colour. It can be hard to define the relationship between colours that you tend to prefer. Being able to describe what you are looking at helps you to distinguish what it is that attracts you to a particular set of colours. The principal attribute of a colour, for example red's 'redness', is known as its 'hue'. Primary hues are red, blue and yellow. Secondary hues are purple, green and orange. There are, of course, many intermediate hues as well, such as a bluish-green.

Triadic colour

Monochromatic colour

Apposite colour

A tint is a hue, such as red, with white added. A shade is a hue with black added. A tone is a hue with grey added. 'Light value' is the amount of light a colour can reflect. All hues can be seen as white at the top of the light value scale and black at the bottom. 'Chroma' is the strength or intensity of a colour. Strong colours have full chroma, weak colours are nearly grey.

Colour, like language, has a sort of grammar. Just as words are combined in sentences to produce different meanings, so colours can be combined to produce particular effects – harmony, contrast, accent.

If you decorate only with hue, you get boldness without subtlety; if only with light value you get a Monochromatic effect: fine variations of tint and shade but no contrast and vitality. Decorate only with chroma and you get a variety of colours but no light and shade.

Colours have been organized as a spectrum (Newton), wheel (Munsell), circle (Steiner), chords (Itten), triangle (Goethe), sphere (Runges) and planes (Eastern theologies) in attempts to explain their relationship with one another.

Finding your colour combinations

A Monochromatic colour combination uses shades of one hue and an Apposite colour combination uses shades of two adjacent hues to produce contrast and variety. The hues can be wholly cool (see the green example) or wholly warm (see the pink combination). Use almost any colour like this and the effect is quiet and subtle, simply because there are no jarring contrasts. Is this soothing, or does it lack excitement?

A Triadic colour combination covers the three extremes of the spectrum. It will always produce two warm and one cool, or two cool and one warm colour. Triadic combinations produce a bold and cheerful effect. Think of the Bauhaus palette of blue, yellow and red, or a kindergarten combination of green, purple and orange. Do you find this cheerful or daring, didactic or unsubtle?

The Complementary colour combination takes two hues on diametrically opposite sides of the spectrum. This way, one will always be warm, and the other cool. It satisfies the eye by supplying the missing colour it expects to see. It balances the books visually. Does this combination satisfy you, or does it seem too straightforward?

Using Accented colour – adding a touch of contrasting colour to two colours that are next to each other on the spectrum – adds bite. This is colour with a pay-off. Could you resist adding an accent colour to an otherwise harmonious room?

Which of these four colour combinations appeals to you the most? Write down the one you prefer.

Understanding your colour combinations

Look at your own home, and recall rooms you have decorated over the years. What colour combinations have you tended to use? Perhaps you grew up in a sea of toning monochromes and now find you need as much colour and contrast as possible.

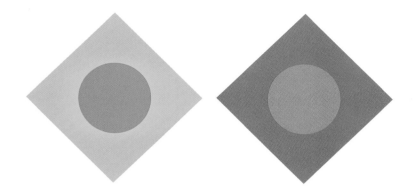

Complementary colour

Accented colour

It can often be easier to see the colour patterns in the rooms of people you know. For instance, someone may have decorated in shades of lilac and turquoise (Apposite colours) as long as you have known them. How muddy or clear the colours are may vary over time, but they always return to the same basic combination. It is not just that they like the cool colours, but this particular combination of colours has some resonance for them. Or a sensation seeker may relish the heat and the clash of red with pink, or purple with red, unrelieved by any third party.

order and chaos

Personal space is not just about what we have, it's also about how we live. Practicalities first – how much order do we need, how much chaos can we take? We take the particular way that we function in our personal space so much for granted that we forget how much this can vary from person to person.

Our organizational habits can be very revealing, and sometimes surprising. Not all surgeons or spacious loft apartments are tidy, any more than artists or family homes are necessarily chaotic. When two people start to share a home, the degree of order and chaos each is prepared to put up with becomes clear within days. Whatever one thought of as normal behaviour (polishing the taps after every use, stockpiling food, keeping tights in the fridge) is thrown into relief by the other's habits.

But judging others against our own standards is not usually helpful. Who is to say whether it is controlling or simply tidy to insist that towels are left on the towel rail rather than on the radiator? If you let your old newspapers pile up on a corner of the dining table are you easy-going or a slob? It is all subjective. In the end the only opinions that matter in this area are your own and those of the people you live with.

To be happy in your own home, you need to make up your mind how acceptable you find your own organizational habits. If it makes you happier to see your friends having a rowdy time than it does to see every surface gleaming, then accept that even aspiring to a purist lifestyle is a waste of effort. Some people barely notice the toothmarks on the sofa because they

love their dogs more than their furniture. If shape, colour and form are in themselves a huge source of pleasure to you, then having beautiful things in your home is an end in itself. It comes down to how perfectible you believe your home can and should be.

Is your tidiness – or lack of it – a reaction to another person in your life? Are you still rebelling against your parents by choosing to live differently from them? If you are still living at home well into adulthood, organizing your room differently to the rest of the space marks it out as a semi-detached household. If your partner is at the opposite end of the order–chaos axis, how much of your behaviour is to prove a point? And are you tidying up after another person because you like things to be tidy or because you do not want them to be there?

Your place on the order–chaos axis

Look at the kitchens in the pictures and choose the one that most reflects the general degree of order in your own home. Write down whether you have chosen the top, middle or bottom picture.

Next read through the following sets of six statements. Copy down the one in each block (A–E) that describes the lifestyle closest to your own.

Look at your five choices as a mini-portrait of yourself. Does it sound like you? What is missing? What are you proud of and what would you change?

A

The laundry basket is usually full

I regularly send clothes to a dry cleaner

My linen cupboard is in good order

I prefer my clothes to dry in the air and sun

I scent my linen drawers

I would rather buy new clothes than keep washing them

B

I cannot bear to see things left on the floor

I have a place for everything

I am always throwing stuff out

I am always rearranging my things attractively

I like to put unexpected things together. If I put something down by chance and it looks good I will leave it there

I often run out of supplies

C

I always rinse dishes twice

I wash up before I go to bed

I wash up after every meal

I wash up in emergencies

I do not mind washing up because warm dishes and foam feel good

Washing up is a penance

D

I always check my bills carefully

I file my bills away

I spend as little time on my bills as possible

I know roughly how big my bills will be

Often I cannot find where I put my bills

I would rather not open my bills, thank you

E

Open shelves may be easy, but I do not like the way they collect dust

I love cupboards with invisible catches

If you have cupboards you will only fill them with junk

I have special places for special objects

There is nothing more depressing than a wall of fitted cupboards

I do not know what is in my cupboards and drawers

indulgence and denial

All of us feel the tension between discipline and luxury, and are aware of the indulgences and comforts we are prepared to live with or without. But what sways us one way rather than the other? When aesthetics matter more than comfort, denial becomes a virtue. We all know someone who can turn self-denial into an art form. The effect can be amazing, which is often the point.

Their simple surroundings seem to turn back the clock, before fitted kitchens, central heating and walk-in closets; their few belongings displayed on pegs like trophies from the 'I can live on less than you' war.

How much we enjoy paring down the business of life to its essentials varies widely from person to person. Many of us feel this urge only in pockets of our lives, banishing ironing entirely, for instance. Others can confuse this with sheer laziness. An urge to purge can come unbidden during major upheavals such as divorce or a death in the family: divesting oneself of the accoutrements of the old life feels like shedding one's skin. On the other hand, holding on to the possessions that evoke a lost life can be an essential stage on the route to eventually moving on. Throwing everything out too soon can be a mistake, only emphasizing how much has been lost.

The number of possessions people like to surround themselves with has waxed and waned over the centuries. Although it can be a simple matter of affluence, it has much to do with dogma: aesthetic or political. Periods of indulgence such as the mid- to late-nineteenth century – notorious for the prodigious quantities of ornaments that were acceptable in one room – have regularly provoked a retreat into austerity. The accretions of junk are sluiced out by purifying movements such as classical revivalism, the International style, and the revival of Shaker style.

The same principle applies to individuals as their fortunes change. Just as a nation in recession can dream of luxury goods and then affect simplicity during a boom, so people in bleak surroundings will feel a strong urge to embellish them. Those with the means to easily fill a room can pare their taste to the bone once an appetite for indulgence becomes distasteful. On moving to a new and larger home, everyone must have had the urge to preserve the expanses of empty space and the competing desire to fill them with familiar objects. How much of your past you wish to carry with you is the crucial issue here.

Your place on the indulgence–denial axis

First look at the bedrooms in the pictures and choose the one that most reflects the general degree of sensual and aesthetic indulgence in your own home. Write down your choice.

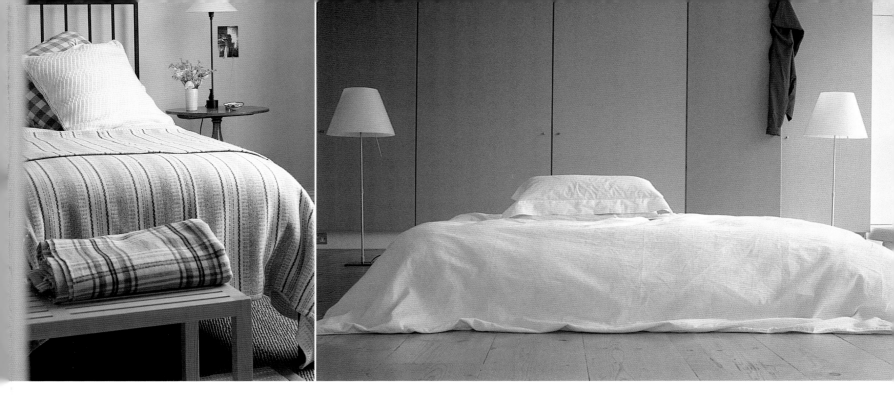

Now read through the following sets of statements. Write down the one in each block (F–J) that describes the lifestyle closest to your own.

When you look at your choices, can you spot any anomalies? Are there any statements that you are a little bit ashamed of? Why?

F

My bed is heaven

My bed is where I sleep

My bed is in keeping with the rest of my home

My bed is where a lot of living goes on

My bed linen is a riot

My bed is my temple

G

I prefer things unscented

Smells do not really register with me

My home has to smell fresh and clean

I regularly develop a passion for different scents

I like my home when it smells sexy; even the whiff of
    bourbon and cigarettes counts

My home has to smell beautiful

H

Silence is golden

I respond to the hum of the city

I have to hear the sounds of nature

I need music to work

Play that music loud, baby

Music should be appropriate

I

Improvised furniture is fine

The less furniture I have the better

I only buy high-quality furniture

Furniture has to be useful before I give it houseroom

Furniture has to look good, first and foremost

Furniture should feel good as well as do its job

J

Food can be design

Food is a necessity

The kitchen is the heart of a home

Food can be amusing

Food can be wicked

Food is an art form

find your place on the personal space spectrum

If you have worked your way through the exercises, you can now find your place on the Personal Space Spectrum. Have your answers to the exercises to hand. These will give you a list of all your favourite things: your ideal home, place, mood and room; the sorts of materials and textures you are drawn to and how you like to arrange them; your favourite colour combinations and a grounding in the everyday realities of how you actually live in your home. This is your personal space file, and it provides you with your key to the Personal Space Spectrum.

By now you might have a good idea as to which of the sensibilities on the Personal Space Spectrum is the closest to your own, but there could be some surprises, too.

Start by looking at the six sectors on page 44–45. Each one contains words that apply to a particular aspect of the Personal Space Spectrum. Taking each sector in turn, check the words against those you have written in your personal space file. Write down all the matching words for each sector on a separate sheet of paper, or tick off each one that matches as you go along.

Words that are very close in meaning count as a match. So, if the sector has a word such as splendid, then an acceptable match could also be splendour, or grandeur or magnificence. Once you have checked your file against every sector, run your eye over the page to see in which sector you have found most matches.

The extracts from four case studies opposite illustrate the sorts of results you may have come up with, although you will probably have produced far more detailed information. Jane's responses to the dream exercises show she is a serious hedonist. Richard's attitude to furnishings and objects is pretty austere. Christopher takes a classical approach to colour, while Isabel thinks of herself as far more domesticated than she really is.

Most people will find all their word matches in one sector. Others may hover on the boundary between two sectors, or even be distributed between two quite separate sectors. Note the sector or sectors that match your answers most closely and turn to pages 46–47 to find a profile of your own sensibility.

This spectrum leads you on to the second half of this book – Create a Personal Space – which provides room-by-room inspiration for each of the six sensibilities. As you will see, each sensibility overlaps, so it can be a good idea to browse through the ideas for adjoining sensibilities, too. And, of course, if your personal space file matches more than one sensibility, look at both. Many of us are of one sensibility by nature, but another by choice. You could be, for instance, Sensuous by nature, but choose to temper your natural inclinations by adopting the discipline of an Urban sensibility.

You can also use the spectrum to help you counteract any tendencies you feel are too extreme. If your responses are heavily in one sector or loaded to one side of the spectrum, then looking at the ideas for creating a personal space on the opposite side of the spectrum may help you to balance your life.

If you can get your partner or family to complete the exercises too, then the results can help illuminate where and why there may be conflict in how you approach your communal space. We often end up living with someone whose sensibility dramatically conflicts with ours. Understanding each other's needs for personal space is an important step on the road to harmony.

CASE STUDIES

Jane

Home Tropical beach hut (exotic, luscious, elemental)
My ideal is a Moroccan hotel I once stayed in – discreet, shady, mysterious. My visualized home is self-indulgent, luxurious, and hidden in greenery. My childhood home was a plain modern house, which I found really bland. The garden was much more exciting.
Place Lake (serene, harmonious, gentle) *I would love a large garden or orchard with lots of distinct areas and a big wall around it.*

Mood Mogul (humid, microcosm, languid) *I also love that decadent idea of Orientalism, although I know it's more fantastical than based on reality. Quiet opulence with a hint of debauchery.*
Room Dining room (richly coloured, comfortable, glittering) *Having a dining room has always seemed like a really indulgent thing to me, I've always had to eat in the kitchen.*
Jane's sensibility: Wild and Sensuous, with an undercurrent of Easy. Perhaps this will become more pronounced as she gets older.

Richard

Texture Concrete (solid, hardcore, robust) *It's just really basic and can take anything you do to it. When it cracks and stains, it shows its history. It's not precious. It's real, and it allows you to have fun. I can't bear precious textiles.*
Pattern Weave (plain, simple, unfussy) *I really prefer solid shapes or massive splurges to little repetitive patterns.*
Ornament Bundled (original, improvised, cheap) *This is quite fun, although I wouldn't bother to do it. I like the way the wire is just wrapped round. I don't like fuss.*

Shape Planes (scientific, abstract, challenging) *I love this because it strips a chair down to its essentials. I wear functional clothes, my body does what it's supposed to, and so should my furniture.*
Arrangement Clutter (themed, spontaneous, memorabilia) *I collect whatever appeals to me. But I don't arrange them as such. Just put them down where they won't get in the way. I think the idea of a mantelpiece display is very bourgeois.*
Richard's sensibility: Pure and Maverick. He probably needs a more fun-loving partner if he is to stop being so doctrinaire.

Christopher

Palette Calm *I find these colours very reassuring and restful. They don't demand anything, they're subtle. I love the soft grey: that looks really Regency to me. An elegant Georgian town house would be painted in these colours. I love them all. They all work as a backdrop to life, and enhance forms such as mouldings and pictures. I wear all these colours too.*
Combination Monochromatic and Apposite *They don't clash, they enhance each other by being so close in tone. I like to decorate a*

room like this so the various shades of one colour balance each other. My drawing room has a mid-green carpet, pale green walls and a very light green ceiling. This way you are gently bathed in the colour, and objects and furniture are enhanced by being seen against a very consistent background. I was brought up in a very classical house, full of antiques and fine fabrics, and I now have an eye for quality.
Christopher's sensibility: a mix of Pure, Easy and Urban. Would react with horror to the more outrageous side of the spectrum.

Isabel

Order and Chaos Bottom kitchen *I'm always in the midst of clearing away one thing and cooking another. My mother was the same, but she was more successful at being tidy than I am. I'd now find a really tidy, cleared-away kitchen rather clinical and off-putting.*
Statement choices My linen cupboard is in good order / I have a place for everything / I wash up before I go to bed / I know roughly how big my bills will be / I have special places for special objects. *This all makes me sound like an old-fashioned*

homebody, which I'm not. I just wish I were. The picture actually tells the truth more than these wishful statements.
Indulgence and Denial Middle bedroom
Statement choices My bed is where I sleep / food is an art form / I prefer things unscented / music should be appropriate. *I sound a bit too uptight for my liking. But I hadn't realized how important food and feeding people is to me.*
Isabel's sensibility: a complicated but easy-to-be-with mix of mainly Wild, Easy and Sensuous.

spectrum diagnoser

Exercise choices

Tower • Foreshore • Zen • Bathroom

Concrete • Weave • Ribbed • Planes
• Asymmetry

Calm • Triadic

Top kitchen • Right bedroom

Statement choices

I prefer my clothes to dry in the air and sun /
I am always throwing stuff out / I wash up after
every meal / I spend as little time on my bills as
possible / If you have cupboards you will only
fill them with junk

My bed is where I sleep / I prefer things unscented
/ Silence is golden / The less furniture I have the
better / Food is a necessity

Key words

original / elemental / meditative / clean /
industrial / quiet / unobtrusive / scientific /
contemplative / ambitious / bracing /
impassive / separate / strong / unadulterated /
moderate / abstract / striking / conceptual /
clean / freeing / secure / solid / basic /
challenging / efficient / demanding

Exercise choices

Ranch house • Market • Morocco • Study

Old paint • Curlicue • Bundled • Spiral
• Clutter

Vibrant • Complementary • Accented

Bottom kitchen • Middle bedroom

Statement choices

The laundry basket is usually full / I like to
put unexpected things together. If I put
something down by chance and it looks good
I will leave it there / Washing up is a penance /
Often I cannot find where I put my bills /
There is nothing more depressing than a wall of
fitted cupboards

My bed linen is a riot / I regularly develop a
passion for different scents / I need music to
work / Improvised furniture is fine / Food can
be amusing

Key words

out of the way / varied / loose / stimulating /
unpredictable / whimsical / original / bizarre /
themed / ramshackle / bustling / informal /
bolstering / sense of history / jolly / cheap /
inventive / intricate / freethinking / amusing /
relaxed / fun / haphazard / mind-boggling /
irregular / refreshing / memorabilia

Exercise choices

Château • Lagoon • Gothic • Dining room

Leather • Damask • Carved • Monumental
• Profusion

Vibrant • Accented

Bottom kitchen • Left bedroom

Statement choices

I would rather buy new clothes than keep
washing them / I often run out of supplies /
I wash up in emergencies / I would rather not
open my bills, thank you / I do not know what is
in my cupboards and drawers

My bed is my temple / I like my home when it
smells sexy; even the whiff of bourbon and
cigarettes counts / Play that music loud, baby /
Furniture has to look good, first and foremost /
Food can be wicked

Key words

grand / intense / florid / indulgent / animal /
warmth / wild / elaborate / stirring / lavish /
impressive / colourful / vulgar / greedy / smells
good / over the top / classical / primitive / rich /
fairy tale / vivid / mad / extravagant / sexy /
complex / regal / grand / stimulating

| pure | maverick | wild |

Exercise choices

Tropical beach hut • Virgin forest • Mogul • Bedroom

Feathers • Tessellate • Teardrop • Curve • Harmony

Warm • Monochromatic • Apposite

Middle kitchen • Left bedroom

Statement choices

I scent my linen drawers / I am always rearranging my things attractively / I don't mind washing up because warm dishes and foam feel good / I know roughly how big my bills will be / I have special places for special objects

My bed is heaven / My home has to smell beautiful / Music should be appropriate / Furniture should feel good as well as do its job / Food is an art form

Key words

exotic / profuse / heady / cosseting / frivolous / lush / attenuated / smooth / balanced / luscious / all-enveloping / languorous / welcoming / light / intricate / curved / billowing / expressive / close to nature / heated / rhapsodic / dreamy / delicate / lulling / fine / inviting / thoughtful

Exercise choices

Cottage • Lake • Shaker • Kitchen

Wool • Stripe • Balled • Angular • Clusters

Warm • Monochromatic • Apposite • Triadic

Middle kitchen • Middle bedroom

Statement choices

My linen cupboard is in good order / I have a place for everything / I wash up before I go to bed / I always check my bills carefully / Open shelves may be easy, but I do not like the way they collect dust

My bed is where a lot of living goes on / My home has to smell fresh and clean / I have to hear the sounds of nature / Furniture has to be useful before I give it houseroom / The kitchen is the heart of a home

Key words

pretty / serene / ordered / hard-working / natural / unaffected / real / crisp / informal / nostalgic / harmonious / unpretentious / nurturing / traditional / straightforward / undisguised / clean / artless / peaceful / gentle / well-crafted / ergonomic / warm / easy / proper / casual

Exercise choices

Penthouse • City • Art Deco • Living room

Perspex • Geometric • Fluted • Fluid • Regularity

Fresh • Calm • Monochromatic • Apposite

Top kitchen • Right bedroom

Statement choices

I regularly send clothes to a dry cleaner / I cannot bear to see things left on the floor / I always rinse dishes twice / I file my bills away / I love cupboards with invisible catches

My bed is in keeping with the rest of my home / Smells do not really register with me / I respond to the hum of the city / I only buy high-quality furniture / Food can be design

Key words

cool / energizing / sharp / sophisticated / modern / regular / delicate / integrated / ordered / funky / powerful / impressive / sociable / clear / restrained / exquisite / elemental / complete / streamlined / hectic / glamorous / fine living / adaptable / minimal / refined / spare / severe

sensuous

easy

urban

easy

A down-to-earth and practical
sensibility. Treasures the simple
pleasures and upholds enduring
values. Appreciates comfort,
but finds sustainable, functional
solutions, much like **urban**.

PERSONAL **SPACE** SPECTRUM **PERSONAL** SPACE **SPECTRUM** PERSONAL **SPACE** SPECTRU

sensuous

Values subtlety and comfort just as
much as indulgence. Knows how
to prolong sensual satisfaction by
balancing it with order and harmony.
Can be nostalgic, as can **easy**.

PERSONAL **SPACE** SPECTRUM **PERSONAL** SPACE **SPECTRUM** PERSONAL **SPACE** SPECTRU

wild

Displays a pronounced taste for
the extreme, the exotic, even
decadent. In love with glamour
and demands stimulation. Ruled
by sensory pleasure, but far more
theatrical than **sensuous**.

chaos

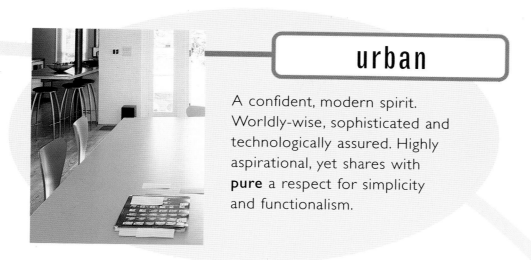

urban

A confident, modern spirit. Worldly-wise, sophisticated and technologically assured. Highly aspirational, yet shares with **pure** a respect for simplicity and functionalism.

PERSONAL SPACE SPECTRUM PERSONAL SPACE SPECTRUM PERSONAL SPACE SPECTRUM

pure

A more rigorous, meditative temperament that relishes the intellectual challenge of pure form and colour. Will put up with inconvenience to achieve results, much like **maverick**.

self denial

ERSONAL SPACE SPECTRUM PERSONAL SPACE SPECTRUM PERSONAL SPACE SPECTRUM

maverick

Always ready to improvise, and ready to explore every whim. Unpretentious and witty, with an eclectic approach. Impact and contrast matter almost as much as they do to **wild**.

create a personal space

Once we understand our own sensibilities better we can begin to explore ways of putting that knowledge to work. The living rooms, kitchens, dining rooms, bedrooms, studies and hallways that appear in this section will provide you with ideas and inspiration, whatever your sensibility. You can turn straight to the relevant sensibility, explore around its fringes, or take a peek at its opposite. Either way, what you come away with will be a unique blueprint for you to use in your own space. It will help you to make a home that fulfils your needs and projects your individuality to the world — your own very personal space.

pure

Austerity is something of an acquired taste for all but the most ascetic temperament. A spiritual awakening can provoke it, or a weariness of over-indulgence, or even a creeping disgust with the general messiness of life, domestic or otherwise. Purifying the living place is an ancient method of concentrating the mind on higher things, but a Pure room can also provide a breathing space, a retreat from a bustling world.

The urge to purify the home is about two things: control and self-denial. Control over objects that seem to multiply of their own accord, over the randomness with which the ordinary home is put together and the potential chaos that threatens to disrupt the best of intentions. And self-denial, in the sense of restricting earthly comforts and consolations, eliminating surplus baggage · and unnecessary indulgences. Tightening one's belt in times of plenty is a corrective measure, not a necessity.

When this reductive urge is motivated by a drive towards greater spirituality, turning one's back on all but the most essential earthly goods involves letting go of supports rather than pushing them away. As an Aboriginal proverb has it, 'the more you know the less you need'.

Zen Buddhism, founded by the Indian Buddhist monk, Daruma, who visited Japan in the sixth century, is based on the idea that experience and expression are one, so the only way to learn is through doing. And because in Zen teaching the home is as much a place for the spirit as for the body,

it emphasizes the spiritual rewards of physical privation. Inner needs become more important than external comfort. What we now think of as the typical traditional Japanese home represents the ultimate austerity in Western eyes: mats instead of furniture, wadded futons in place of beds, and flimsy partitions providing none of the privacy of solid walls.

Zen rooms emphasize natural textures and contrasts, prize clean, straight, spare lines, and exclude the curve (and its implied sensuality). Ornamentation is deliberately omitted, and furniture is placed in the centre of the room to maintain an unobstructed line. Heinrich Engel wrote that a room in a Western home is 'human without man's presence, for man's memory lingers in the multiple devices of decoration, furniture and utility. A room in a Japanese residence becomes human only through man's presence. Thus, the empty room provides the very space where man's spirit can move freely and where his thoughts can reach the very limits of potential.'

But Pure is not always about heightening inner awareness. It can be a fleeing from

Left and far left, top T. E. Lawrence's Book Room at Cloud's Hill, where he hosted manly picnics for his airforce chums of all ranks. He had two sleeping bags, embroidered with the words Meum and Teum. Teum was for his guests, who stayed in the Bunk Room (far left, top).

Far left, below A Pure room can calm as well as concentrate the mind, as a place in which to enjoy what John Pawson calls the 'uncomplicated beauty of the unadorned wall'.

intolerable sensations. A cluttered room sometimes can be too busy to live in. The film director David Lynch describes the rooms he creates on film in terms of how agitating, or 'fast' they are, on a scale of one to ten: 'an empty room is a two, a person is around a seven, fire and electricity can go up to nine. A really intricately designed, decorative room is pretty disturbing sometimes, it's too fast.' A Pure room provides a breathing space, a retreat, temporary or otherwise, from a world of perceived chaos or mundanity. Stripping down your life is a common reaction to extreme stress. It is the next best thing to simply walking out.

Pure is also motivated by aesthetics – highly sensitive to form, colour and function. But as the flip side of the Sensuous sensibility, Pure is concerned with aesthetic control rather than expression. In his book *Minimum*, British architect John Pawson celebrates what he calls the uncomplicated beauty of the unadorned wall. He built a house for architect Claudio Silvestrin in Majorca, which, with its high, enclosing ochre walls and vast, empty interiors, has all the calm austerity of a monastery. Pawson acknowledges the influence on his aesthetic of the monumental nineteenth-century mills that surround his home town of Halifax in North Yorkshire, England, with their rhythmic, stark façades. In the process of reducing, condensing and excluding what is inessential and therefore trivial, he goes through a mirror, he says, like Alice in Wonderland, which turns the world inside out – emptiness becomes fullness.

The pursuit of Purity honours earlier and simpler times, cultures and places, and often expresses a deep if muscular romanticism, even an exulting sensuality. These values are embedded in Cloud's Hill in Dorset, the derelict cottage that British military adventurer and writer Thomas Edward Lawrence restored after his return to England in 1923.

Lawrence had spent his best years in the Middle East fighting for Arab independence from the Turks (a period immortalized by Peter O'Toole as Lawrence in David Lean's film, *Lawrence of Arabia*). He enthusiastically adopted Arab dress and the nomadic culture, which valued freedom over possessions, and in which ability conferred the sole status. 'For years we lived anyhow with one another in the naked desert, under the indifferent heaven,' Lawrence recalled in *The Seven Pillars of Wisdom*. 'By day the hot sun fermented us, and we were dizzied by the beating wind. At night we were stained by dew, and shamed into pettiness by the innumerable silences of stars.'

Although his political ambition waned and he retired from public life, he continued to worship fervently all that was free, fierce and unforgiving, comradely and heroic. Cloud's Hill is a static monument to the nomadic camp spirit Lawrence loved. Over its door he inscribed a Greek phrase of indifference to worldly status. 'It means', he wrote, 'that nothing in Cloud's Hill is to be a care upon its inhabitant. While I have it, there shall be nothing exquisite or unique in it. Nothing to anchor me.'

For the wooden-floored and -beamed Book Room, he designed a simple leather-covered divan and pillow. The Bunk Room was lined with metal and lit by a porthole. Today Lawrence's three glass domes, in which he kept his bread, cheese and butter, are to be found there. Days before his death, he wrote of Cloud's Hill: 'It is an earthly paradise and I am staying here until I feel qualified for it.'

Left In Zen homes, extraneous ornamentation is deliberately excluded, except for the art alcove (*tokonoma*) and small low shelf (*chiga-dana*). Rice-paper windows (*shoji*) diffuse the variations in light throughout the day, giving the effect of permanent afternoon.

Far left Pure is preoccupied with what will endure and is of lasting value; what will not date; and the reassurance that a material or structure or colour goes beyond what is immediately obvious.

Below John Pawson in his minimalist kitchen in London. 'It was', he reveals, 'a sense of the oppressive weight of possession that gave me my first taste for simplicity.'

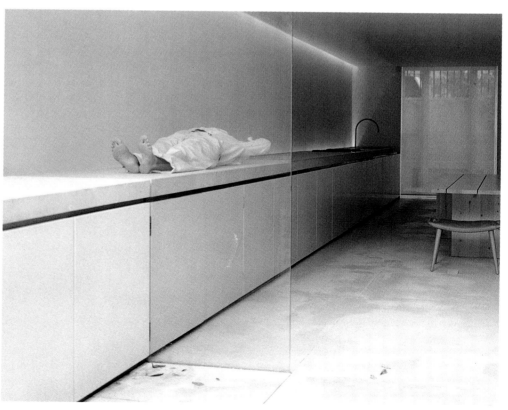

the pure living room

This is as much a place for contemplation as a space for living. This room should be both soothing and uplifting, and designed to offer a welcome rigour. Only introduce something if you are certain of its necessity. The Japanese respect the space between objects, and the flow of this space, which will be affected by what you acquire. Think of how the boulders in a Japanese garden are arranged: with space to breathe but with a circling interdependence.

Right The sense of balance is very powerful in this room: planes and forms echo and contrast in a balanced asymmetry. The cupboard sets off the coffee table, while the long sofas facing each other have a direct relationship. Floor-to-ceiling blinds provide a soft, diffuse light, similar to that of Japanese rice-paper windows (*shoji*), which make everything seem dreamily perfect. And, while there is some element of clutter, the books and pot are mere droplets in an ocean of pure form. Every large piece of furniture is freestanding, allowing the space to flow freely.

Above Position a bench or day bed by the largest window, and find time to sit there regularly. You will find that you heighten your awareness of both shelter and exposure, and balance the interior world with the outer. This particular day bed, a large wooden cradle, offers an unusual combination of security and stringency.

the pure kitchen

Of all domestic tasks, food preparation creates the most fuss, debris and paraphernalia. But even this can be tamed within the Pure sensibility. Build a rigorously substantial and low-maintenance shell that, while retaining a practical workplace for cooking at home, is as neutral and fuss-free as possible. Then if you want to make a ritual out of your cooking, there will be nothing to distract you – and very little to clear up afterwards.

Below The long slab of this island work unit has a commanding presence, and appears to hover mid-room like a sacrificial altar. Backlighting the alcove provides a shrine-like setting for the hob. Making stools out of solid chunks of wood means that they look like a part of the work-unit structure when pushed underneath the eating bar.

Left This rough carcass of a kitchen with its bulwark lamps is virtually maintenance-free. Concrete may stain, but it is solid and virtually indestructible. (If you are adding concrete to a wooden structure, however, make sure it can take the added weight.) If you have open shelves, try not to rack them up conventionally: treat them as pure forms and arrange accordingly. The stainless steel in this kitchen might prove impractical, as the surface needs frequent polishing to keep its unblemished finish.

the pure bathroom

Cleanliness is next to godliness in the Pure bathroom. Bathrooms designed at the height of the vogue to maximize health and efficiency in the 1920s and 1930s took a strictly utilitarian approach, involving much white tile and ceramic. These bathrooms could be breathtakingly small. Happily, modern innovations such as reinforced glass and powerful electric water pumps allow the bathroom to function on a far grander scale, becoming a veritable temple to purification.

Right Here the shower cubicle is so substantial that it takes on the proportions of a room. It offers a sense of freedom that is the next best thing to showering under a waterfall. Site your shower head as high as you can to feel the full force of the water. Setting the controls so far from the shower head also makes strolling into the flow a ritual experience. As steam mists the glass, the intense blue of the wall panels blurs into an inky oceanic background. Again, there is an unencumbered view to the outside world.

Above Setting this stunning, glass square bath at an angle to the walls concentrates the eye firmly on the churning turquoise chunk of water it contains. The slatted table is also starkly linear and can fold away to allow the bather to enjoy the simple pleasures of light, air and water unencumbered. Hidden channels allow the water to drain away invisibly.

Right This is a back-to-basics bathroom. Unadorned and rough-hewn wood is used here to imposingly dramatic effect. Strong horizontal slabs of timber, supported by monolithic struts, give the effect of bathing in a barn. The contrast with the bath, basin and taps, all in the classic tradition, couldn't be greater. A bathroom like this will look even better with age, since the wood is already well-seasoned.

Above Massively bulky or expensive materials aren't essential. Here, the simple and traditional device of a wall painted in subtle, yet contrasting, colours creates a serene and utilitarian air. Blocking in the bath with plain ply or medium density fibreboard works too, as long as it is well finished. Otherwise, the key is to do as little to the room as possible. The rafters have been left untouched, and the old cabinet unrestored, leaving the simple towel rail as the only strong presence.

the pure bedroom

The simplest sleeping arrangement is to lie under the stars on bare ground. The Pure bedroom echoes this spartan ideal by sticking to its three basic elements – bed, floor and open space. Beyond providing a place of repose, it should either make use of local materials, or make one grand sculptural statement. Isolating the bed in the centre of the room gives it the requisite gravitas. Any art should be along the lines of a James Turrell light painting, any patterns should be natural or geometric.

Left Although the round bed is associated with Hollywood excess and vulgarity, this variation on the theme encloses it within a flowing spiral form, perfectly attuned to the requirements of curled sleeping bodies. It is the nest made abstract, a secure enclosure that, if anything, carries more primitive resonance than the conventional bed. For it to work well, the room around it should be kept as empty as possible.

Below The dramatic yet unaffected wall of darkest blue is an eloquent invitation to deep sleep. Japanese beds can be rolled up and put away during the day, and this dazzling white duvet seems to conceal little more than the floor. The reflective floor itself enhances the sense that the low bed is floating. The room appears to be permanently open to other areas of the house, and the bed could just as well be laid down somewhere else.

Right Textures, colours and materials have all been dictated by the shell of this space: everything fits with the varied hues of natural stone, wood and plaster. The linen is as simple as possible, and the bed itself is low, although its enormous bulk goes some way to contradict such humble garb.

the pure hall

A perfectly unadorned entrance hall will set a peaceful tone for the rest of the home, and will calm senses overstimulated by the outside world. The Japanese entrance lobby developed as a place for guests to leave their shoes, so that they would not sully the floor on which they would sit as well as walk. As a symbolic gesture, this also reflects a resolve to keep the home free from traces of the exterior world. If your entrance opens directly into a room, install a screen to mark the change in pace.

Right In such a starkly geometric configuration, details such as the alignment of floorboards are critical to the success of the whole scheme. To ensure the line is true, new floorboards could replace or be laid over old, irregular boards. Picking one wall out in a darker colour and balancing it with the dark table emphasizes volume and angle. Above all, keep the lines sharp and clean; any whisper of poor workmanship and the whole thing will have to be redone.

Right This ancient stairway could have been painted entirely in white, but leaving bare all the wooden elements of banister, beams and skirting has more integrity. The pale green urn in the alcove provides an unobtrusive focal point: anything more emphatic would be a mistake. Using traditional local materials, such as whitewash, enhances the connection with the past.

maverick

Samuel A. Maverick was a nineteenth-century cattle rancher who became famously annoying when, for his own reasons, he refused to brand his cattle like everyone else and let them roam with every appearance of being God's own creatures. He was just the sort of quirky character who would appeal to any congenital nonconformist. Whether the Maverick spirit is born of sheer obstinacy, unquenchable originality or considered opposition, conformity is not an option.

The Maverick will go his or her own way no matter what, and will manage to insinuate individuality into the most conventional establishment. When America's third president, the multitalented Thomas Jefferson, built his own house at Monticello, Virginia, USA, he designed a bed to fit in the wall between the study and bedroom so he could roll out into either room according to whim.

Mavericks invest a home with talismanic significance. Their home is an aesthetic statement, not for display, but in the sense of remaking the physical world in order to reflect their own inner world. It becomes a place of dreams, a spiritual retreat from inner turmoil and external distraction; what the British writer Virginia Woolf called a 'vessel' that kept her afloat, buoyed up her trajectory and kept her dreams alive.

Woolf claimed to have no aesthetic sense for decoration or fashion, but the visual acuteness evident in her work is equally obvious in her country home, a cottage known as Monk's House in Rodmell, Sussex. To concentrate on her writing, she would retreat to an

austerely furnished lodge built against the garden wall, moving the desk around occasionally to gain a different view. She slept in a simple single bed under the window with stacks of books on shelves in an alcove at her head. Intelligent conversation was her lifeblood, and she made a ritual of teatime with friends in the intense mineral green sitting room, installing comfortable chairs to host long evenings by the fire. Decorative flourishes in fabric, tiles and paint were provided by her sister Vanessa Bell and the painter Duncan Grant.

The Bloomsbury Group, of which Woolf was a central member, kept itself afloat on a self-referential raft of intellectual association and artistic intimacy. Another vessel for creativity was Charleston, a farmhouse four miles away from Monk's House. In 1916 Vanessa Bell and her children, along with Duncan Grant and his friend David Garnett, took over the conventional and unloved house. They extended and remodelled it, eventually decorating practically every surface – fire surrounds, lamp bases, gramophone

Below left and bottom left The apparent folly of making a Japanese-style garden out of a windswept pebble beach posed an irresistible challenge to Derek Jarman. If conventional wisdom dictates that one should do one thing, the Maverick is impelled to do otherwise.

Below Vanessa Bell and her friends remodelled Charleston, decorating practically every surface with stencil designs and distinctive brushwork.

cabinets, bath panels, splashbacks – with their own stencil designs and loose brushwork. They also filled the house with painted ceramics, cross-stitch cushions and printed fabrics.

Vanessa's granddaughter, Virginia Nicholson, remembers the house as a place where 'creativity was a way of life. Paint and clay, mud, glue and matches were all endlessly available... There is a wonderfully uninhibited, irreverent quality to the decoration of the house which is that of a child let loose to experiment and which is extraordinarily liberating... What if the surfaces were not properly prepared? What if there was rising damp? Duncan and Vanessa were undaunted by such considerations. Their creative wells never showed any signs of drying up, so if the tabletop decorations wore out, they could always paint new ones on top.'

The Maverick's forte is intelligent aesthetics. Imagination and ideas are more important to the Maverick sensibility than comfort or conformity, even received notions of aptness or quality. The architect Robert Venturi, who rebelled against Mies van der Rohe's 'less is more' with the motto 'less is a bore', described the (at the time) controversial house he built in 1964 for his mother in Philadelphia, as 'using a joke to get to seriousness'. From the outside it looks like a wry take on an ordinary child's drawing of a generic suburban home, and inside are odd juxtapositions of scale and quirky touches such as open stairs which eat into the chimney breast. 'I am for messy vitality over obvious unity,' he wrote, 'the difficult unity of inclusion rather than the easy unity of exclusion.'

The Maverick requires a home environment that is a place of variety and nourishment, while fighting shy of the overstimulating and indulgent. The more inclusive the taste, the more room there is for wit and juxtaposition, and even kitsch.

The British artist and filmmaker Derek Jarman immersed himself in a more eclectic social circle than did the Bloomsbury set, but his output was just as varied and voluminous. One friend called him 'an egomaniacal jellyfish floating on the warm currents of the world's oceans'. He had a political and aesthetic conscience, protesting against the hypocritical and the banal, yet he was no absolutist: his work, like his homes, was full of chance effects. 'I don't suffer from perfectionism,' he once explained. 'The thing is, you mustn't be precious about things, and then you can get a lot done.'

Jarman turned all his homes into low-tech, high-impact environments. In 1987 he bought Prospect Cottage, a fisherman's beach hut at Dungeness, Kent. He replaced the windows and painted them yellow, and daubed one wall with poems written in tar. Gradually he surrounded it with arrangements of found stone and driftwood. Jarman also crammed massive pieces of furniture made from monolithic slabs of wood into his tiny council flat in Charing Cross Road, London, turning the room into a giant adventure playground.

Out on the margins is where Mavericks belong; venture too close to the mainstream and they fall from glory. The Bloomsbury aesthetic, at the time a manifestation of the eccentricity of a privileged few, has since been assimilated by nostalgia into the rather more conventional upper-class taste known as shabby chic. Robert Venturi's house looks little more than cheeky today. The jury is still out on Jarman.

Left Mavericks are born beachcombers. The variety of styles in this room is bewildering – concrete floor and industrial storage shelving mixed with a untility cupboard, and squabbed wooden dining chairs painted with a metallic finish, rounded off with a fat floral armchair and an array of ornaments – but the fullness and exuberance of such an all-encompassing eye keeps the room alive with resonances.

the maverick living room

Treat this as your playroom: you can do what you like with it. Just keep the space flexible and informal enough to accommodate spontaneous parties, all-night projects and your latest enthusiasms. The state of the shell isn't important, it's what you fill it with that counts. Introduce whatever you fancy: let your eye be the unifying factor. Then, keep rearranging until it feels right.

Above Cherished – if a little battered – objects are the focus of this room. The recently re-covered chaise and chair, and the lampshade keep it looking fresh. A perfect place for every piece can always be found, so keep repositioning if something does not look quite right. Rooms don't need to be themed; let your eclectic jumble ramble through the home, setting you off on a voyage of discovery. Exploit the atmospheric possibilities of small rooms and odd corners by setting up small collections of linked items at every turn.

Below The huge mirror propped up against the wall, the random assortment of windows and unfinished plastering, would upset a tidiness fanatic, but for a Maverick these elements simply add visual interest. As your eye roams about this room, some new alignment or angle inevitably catches your attention, since a Maverick, like a jackdaw, is attracted to all kinds of unexpected treasures. There will always be another irresistible object to add, so the larger the space, the better.

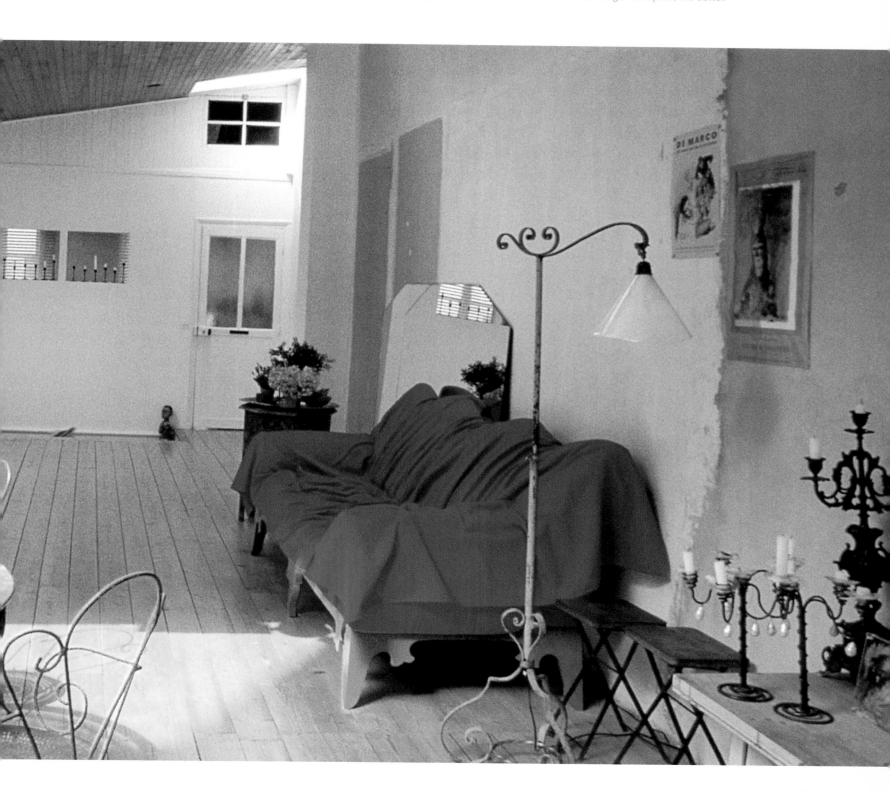

the maverick kitchen

Not being too hung up on achieving optimum efficiency or tidiness frees you to create your own atmosphere by finding witty solutions to given situations. Avoid the obvious answer and think laterally, or take a theme and push it to the hilt. A well-stocked kitchen is a visual cacophony of labels, colours and shapes anyway, so exploit what is naturally there. Just let your imagination go – make the kitchen a vibrant expression of individual personality.

Right The unique style of this galley kitchen, a mix of custom-built and utility, comes from simple materials combined in an unusual way, together with a splash of something fancy in the moulded ply. The units are an ingenious meld of wire mesh, pegboard and ply, with sliding panels and drawers. Ranging the retro appliances together on the right emphasizes their bulbous forms. Panels of colour on the floor (echoed in the coloured fluorescent strip lights) are just for fun, but playfully emphasize the delineation of space.

Above If something appeals, like this vinyl and chrome 1950s dining set, then buy it: it will give you far more pleasure than a safe choice ever could. Surround yourself with the well-loved belongings that you have been unable to resist. This kitchen has a strong retro flavour, but jumbles up its periods so it avoids being too precious.

Right The rough-and-ready approach frees up overprescriptive spaces. This kitchen has been loosened up just enough to take it beyond country-style cliché. The stripped wood has been left unstained and the door of the tall cupboard has become an impromptu doodling space. It would be easy to change if you got bored: just repaint in a dark shade. More open shelves can be added as needed, without worrying about whether they will 'fit in'. Always allow room for impulse buys, like this bargain pile of oranges on the worktop.

Above This *ad hoc* kitchen could be set up almost anywhere. It's basic but naturally hygienic – high shelves, wipe-clean table and uncluttered floor – and will adapt to hosting a lively supper party as easily as to solitary newspaper reading or even full-scale dressmaking. The fragment of ornate mantelshelf with its displayed objects rescues the room from becoming totally spartan.

the maverick bathroom

Getting naked in a Maverick bathroom can be like slipping into another world. A bathroom with a lock on the door is the perfect place to escape into your personal fantasy kingdom. Fill the room with miscellaneous artefacts and treasures, or with the key elements of your favourite style, material or colour, and make bathing a conceptual feast. This room should set your mind buzzing in the morning – some of the best ideas come when you're brushing your teeth.

Right The overuse of stencilling and paint effects has given these techniques a bad name but here, simple crescents and minarets, sparsely and strategically placed, pull the Moroccan theme together beautifully. These lanterns and mirrors are unique and wonderful pieces, set casually against a rough background. While each element has great character, the approach is not about showcasing individual items but creating a total effect.

Right Why not cover a tatty floor with outdoor decking? Why not build a cupboard out of what's left over? Why not mount the taps on a slab of wood rather than drill into the wall? Or use another plank as a bath table? As long as the plumbing functions well, you can do what you like with a bathroom. Choose the right skip and it may end up costing you very little, too.

the maverick bedroom

Left This room captures the ambience of a seasoned traveller's habitual resting place. The unusual appliqué world map bedspread sets the scene, together with a skilfully painted *trompe l'oeil* swagged canopy mural. The mural painter has worked around the room, happily oblivious to light switches and cable in a way that would make a more fastidious temperament cringe. The mineral-green shade of paint is not for the tender-hearted either, and the great bamboo-style bed has real character. All in all, a perfect example of healthy haphazardry.

The bedroom should buoy up your dreams, waking or sleeping. It is the place to set free those ideas that would overwhelm other rooms. Indulge in elaborate whimsy and nostalgia, and display the belongings you would only wish to show to intimates. Change it around as soon as the arrangement becomes stale, or if the room fails to lift your mood when you enter it. Physical comfort is not your sole concern: stirring the spirit is paramount.

Right While far simpler in every respect than the global meltdown opposite, this room shows a similar discrimination in the precision of details: plain, pale blankets are balanced with a traditional striped ticking and rich red, floor-to-ceiling curtains. The hi-fi has been contained in the plainest of wooden cubes, allowing flowers and a single ornament to dominate.

the maverick hall

This is your general repository: where you can put all the things that have never found a place elsewhere in the home, and where new finds are kept while you make up your mind what to do with them. If you can make the hall a stopping-off place, especially on the way back from the garden or terrace, all the better. Sitting here for a while provides different perspectives on the rest of your home.

Right Even at Charleston the halls and corridors were left undecorated, but there is no reason why you cannot let your taste spill over from the main rooms. Here, the scattering of elegant bentwood and carved chairs encourage an atmosphere of aching nostalgia to pervade both the corridor and the room beyond. Hanging pictures in informal groups makes it easy to rearrange or add to them when you get bored. As ramshackle as the walls and ceiling may get, what matters is the sense of moving through a personally evocative space.

Above This small, plainly painted lobby, filled with a variety of rustic and ethnic slatted furniture, makes a suitably low-tech setting for the extraordinary painted heads mounted on the wall. Here it is the forms and materials rather than colour that provide the interest. Note that the Maverick doesn't have to adhere to any notions of cultural authenticity: fakes and substitutions are equally acceptable.

Right A limited range of faded, dusty colours and distressed, powdery textures conjures up a whole interior world. A few minutes at this desk will immerse you in a private web of associations and responses. If you sit at your desk regularly enough, this internal map will make far more sense to you than any formal filing system. Just do not allow anyone else to tidy up for you.

the maverick study

A study is the quintessential Maverick place: even if there is not enough space to devote an entire room to your work, dedicate the best spot you have to feeding your imagination. All you need is a desk, a chair and somewhere to store and display notes, works in progress and items that inspire. British writer Alan Bennett stripped the walls of his study and stained them the same green as his father used at his childhood home. Do whatever means the most to you.

Left This extremely simple arrangement of home-office furniture actually serves its purpose very well. Open shelves are best for keeping whatever matters to you most in the forefront of your mind. An L-shaped desk and swivelling chair allow you to move between concentrated study and taking the long view.

wild

Does it quicken the pulse? Does it give you a buzz? Do your pupils dilate when you see it? The defining characteristic of a Wild home is that it excites physical lust. Lust for what it contains, or evokes, or provokes. Wild will try anything once, and is anything but domesticated. Coming home should be as good as going out, and settling down is just another way of getting high.

Wild's lack of restraint leads either to overload, or chaos, or both. No matter what the object of its enthusiasm may be, it is intense. Clash and stimulation take priority over harmony, rest or order. Even to read Lady Sackville-West's description of the Brighton room she decorated for her daughter, Vita, society novelist and lover of Virginia Woolf, takes nerves of steel: 'Her walls are of shiny emerald green paper. Floors green; doors and furniture sapphire blue; ceiling apricot colour. Curtains blue and inside curtains yellowish. The decoration of the furniture mainly beads of all colours painted on the blue ground; even the door-plates are treated the same. I have bright orange pots on her green marble mantelpiece and there are salmon and tomato colour cushions and lampshades. Pictures by Bakst, George Plank and Rodin, framed in passe-partout ribbons.'

When Wild chooses furniture, fixtures and furnishings, the emotional reaction they provoke is all that matters. If it makes them feel good – grander, more sensual, important, individual, outrageous, richer – they have to have it. Unlike Mavericks, who create

environments that make it easier to live in their heads, Wild is impelled to live out a fantasy at home. Turning the impossible dream into a reality is the whole point of the exercise.

Excess becomes a matter of honour. Why have less, asks Wild, genuinely puzzled, when you can have more? Wild opts for shock value, enjoys the childish *frisson* of the absurd and disgusting; defeats banality by piling exaggeration upon exaggeration, multiplying the ordinary to the point where it becomes extraordinary. If Wild conceives a conceit, it must be taken to its logical conclusion: witness the San Francisco woman who has commissioned mosaic artist Jason Mecier to decorate the walls of a three-floor stairway entirely in various pencils.

French artist, writer and long-time opium addict Jean Cocteau led a pretty nomadic life. But, like all vagabonds, as he wrote, 'I am obsessed with property.' Wherever he did settle, he turned his home into a spectacle, overflowing with *objets d'art* and souvenirs. His first personal space was a tiny Parisian apartment, which he lined with theatrically

Above Hearst's grandiosity echoes that of folly builders throughout history, from Lord Berners to Victor Hugo, who wrote *Les Misérables* in a gothic monstrosity on Guernsey.

Left The portrait of William Randolph Hearst that hangs in the library at Hearst Castle is the only one ever painted.

red fabric and where he put up a blackboard for messages just like those found backstage at the theatre. His only real home was an eighteenth-century stone house at Milly-la-Forêt near Fontainebleau, which, from 1947, he shared with actor Jean Marais and later Edouard Dermit.

It is an intense, private world that starts at the garden gate. The salon contains a stuffed cock, a gilded faun and two gilded palm trees. The library is reached via a spiral staircase carpeted in leopard print. 'He installed a desk in his bedroom,' recalled a friend, 'covered with a 'leopard-skin fabric, above which he hung his mementos, but this was not his real work space. He wrote throughout the house: in the salon, where he left papers, notes and drawings all over the place; sometimes in the garden, near the two stone sphinxes; or on the little bridge over the stream.' It was a home so suffused with its owner's individuality that it became an extension of his personality. 'I inhabit this house,' Cocteau wrote, 'I haunt this bric-a-brac.'

Extravagant French decorator Alberto Pinto was inspired to dedicate a suite in his apartment to Cocteau in the 1980s. It contains Cocteauesque wall paintings, a lacquered bedhead, zebra bedspread and cushion cover printed with monkey heads.

The Wild sensibility flourishes in periods and places of economic excess: the decadence of the 'Naughty Nineties', Hollywood in the 1930s, New York in the 1980s, Dubai at the turn of the twenty-first century. The English upper classes have always excelled at it, especially the frivolous set that surrounded the self-promoting Sitwell triumvirate, Edith, Osbert and Sacheverell, in the 1920s and 1930s. A sample dining room: silver-and-aquamarine-lamé-lined walls, with silvered grotto furniture set on marble linoleum.

Flamboyant individuals who became stupendously successful have created exceptional paradises of Wildness: Presley's Graceland, Idi Amin's palaces. Hearst Castle, set in a remote hilltop location known as 'The Enchanted Hill' in San Simeon, California, is perhaps the most fantastical of all. It was designed for media magnate and art collector William Randolph Hearst by the first female architecture graduate of the Ecole des Beaux Arts, Julia Morgan, has 115 rooms and took over 25 years to build. The first section to go up, in 1919, was a mile-long pergola. 'This is the way God probably would have done it if he had had the money,' declared Hearst's weekend guest George Bernard Shaw.

Hearst ended up with the biggest private zoo in the world and a Gothic, Moorish extravaganza of a home that was also earthquake proof. For the ascetic Morgan, dealing with a man who, while travelling in Europe at the age of ten, is reputed to have told his mother he would like to live at Windsor Castle, and then asked her to buy the Louvre, would not have been easy. Morgan's reply to one of Hearst's changeable and preposterous suggestions is typically bold: 'I like your idea for the combination indoor pool and orchid greenhouse. It should be very tropical and exotic. There could be a plate-glass partition in the pool, and the alligators, sharks, etcetera, could disport themselves on one side of it, and visitors could unsuspectingly dive towards it.' Instead, they settled on a huge, indoor 'Roman' mosaic pool with 22-carat gold tiles, which took seven years to complete. As Cocteau put it: 'the essential tact in daring is to know how far one can go too far'.

Above Cocteau filled his house with images of those he loved – drawings, sketches, photographs and paintings – creating an illusory gallery that, if anything, was more powerful than the subjects' human presence.

Right Excess must be matched with excess if it is to be successful. Only the Wild sensibility has the nerve to live with such boldness and not be overwhelmed.

the wild living room

If this is to be a room full of things you cannot resist and yet that retains some coherence, first you must decide on a visual theme. Create a strong frame on an ambitious scale, with a prominent sense of drama. Emphasize height and exaggerate proportion wherever possible. Lay down broad strokes, concentrating on one bold idea: a colour, a shape, a material. This can be embellished over the years without disintegrating entirely. It is a juggling act, so rely on your eye and don't lose momentum.

Right Dark, but definitely not sober. Juxtaposition is the theme here, of the modern and the traditional. The ampersand trademark, wittily inserted in place of the family portrait over the fireplace, says a great deal about the owners' individual tastes. The unadorned, stained panelling grounds the modernity of the cream leather Barcelona chairs, while the carved relief panels find an echo in the zebra stripes and the ornate gilt firescreen and irons.

Above The height of this room has an inherent drama. Cream, beige and warm red provide a classic luxury colour combination, and the materials themselves do not have to be expensive. In addition, orange linings to the blinds and curtains intensify daylight. Note the paired wall-lights and table lamps: doubling up is a reliable trick for instant grandeur. Finally, louvre cupboards solve storage problems without looking too plain or too pastiche.

Right A rock star's living room has to have all the impact of an auditorium. Here a sheer glass wall displays the inner wantonness to the world. Every surface is moulded, reflective or coloured to quite a disorientating degree: you feel you could run up the walls and over the ceiling. Although incredible amounts of money have obviously been lavished on this huge room, installing the same elements in any large space will achieve a similar effect: a bar, free-form seating and intense lighting.

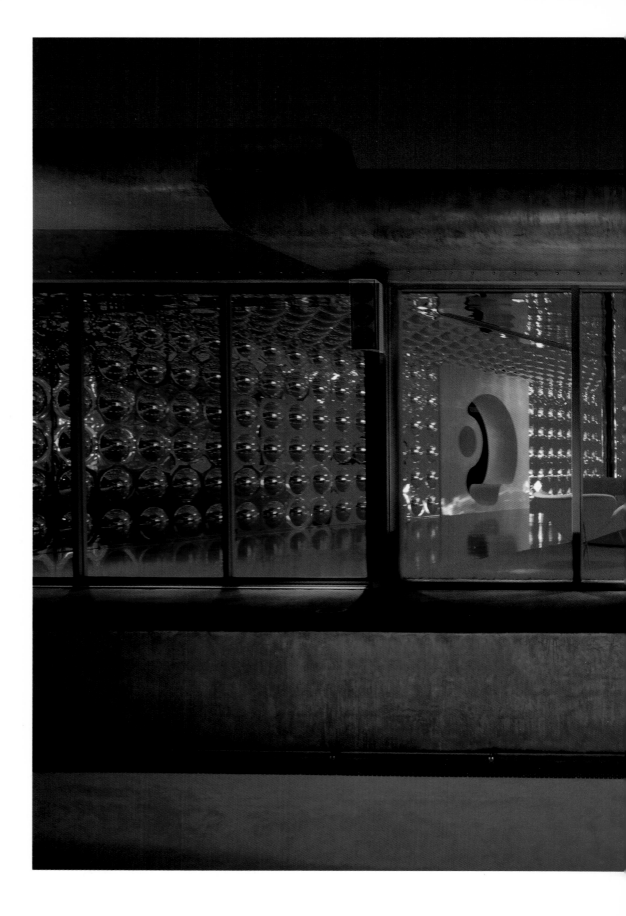

the wild dining room

As the stage for the human theatre of a dinner party, the dining room has the potential to be an extraordinary scene setter. Few people now have time to lay on course after course, so the setting has to carry most of the evening's drama – until the conversation takes off. To emphasize a meal's ritual, the traditional dining set of tables and chairs really comes into its own. In the truly Wild dining room, eating a platter of grapes can be a luxurious experience.

Above Austerity can be dramatic when its historic resonance is exploited. Here, stone walls and a huge fireplace evoke baronial feasts (if these were entirely fake, they would still have a sense of drama and be, if anything, more fun). The deep pile checked carpet that looks like tiling is witty, and luxurious underfoot too. Dining with a flourish requires generosity in all things, even the size of the tablecloth.

Left The heavily swagged table of Nicky Haslam's 1980s dining room is painfully reminiscent of Princess Diana's wedding dress, but his camp neo-baroque style is pure Wild in its wilful ostentation. An arch, knowing homage to the *ancien régime*, its element of illusion is easily punctured. The buffet groans with antique pewter and the clock is permanently set at the time the mob stormed Versailles, but the clouded wall panels are mere tin foil.

the wild bathroom

The bathroom is usually a relatively small room, and busy schemes are too overwhelming, even for a Wild sensibility. Concentrate on opulent materials and dramatic lighting, in the knowledge that your own body is a crucial part of the spectacle. Use lots of mirrors and reflective surfaces, such as polished stone, shiny metal and ceramic. It should look as unclinical as possible (unless you want to pastiche a space-age cosmetics salon, in which case feel free to fetishize anything medical).

Right There is a strong sense of expectancy here. With any luck, something deliciously bad is about to happen. Strong cold colours hint at Weimar and Oriental decadence. The unearthly, acid blue of the walls is unsettling, yet deeply flattering to the skin. Sombre blue wainscotting merges with the shiny black underbelly of the bath to leave bare feet wading in a mysterious dark void. The tall mirror over the clawfoot bath flanked by twin urns would enhance the macabre feeling of stepping into an open coffin.

Right Walls and surfaces are covered with rich marbling, with echoes of the classic early twentieth-century hotel bathroom, where generosity of scale and materials helped to make up for the primitive plumbing. There need be no difference in style between the bathroom and the ballroom; the idea is not to feel stripped but cosseted, and so mirrors should flatter, not revealing too much. There are no utilitarian materials here whatsoever: the mirror is gilded; the chandeliers drip with crystal; the trio of containers are in fluted silver.

the wild bedroom

Left Blue and white in another context make for a dainty bedroom, but this is something different: bedroom as performance venue, where you buy into a myth for the night. Ceilings are important for added stimulation: here globes of light are reflected in a mirrored arch. The great, clean block of a headboard suggests power and strength – no bedside table for book and cocoa, here. Mussing up this downy white and perfect bedlinen has a particular thrill.

For bedroom read playroom. This is primarily a place for sex, so avoid monotony at all costs. Unexpectedness is the key: if the rest of your home is dark or cluttered, make the bedroom light or empty. Hit a new note, open up the vista, make it anything but a dead end. Think of the sexiest place you have ever been and work out what makes it so. Make it robust, though. Nothing around you should be too fragile: you need to be free to move.

Right This is a room for kicking off your shoes and dancing around in. It has a welcoming, slightly retro feel, with curvaceous bedhead, stool and light. The fake fur bed throw and orange 'POP' cushions are exciting but unthreatening. The changing views and light from the floor-to-ceiling windows ensure this room is never dull. It is a great combination of the artificial and natural. Equip it with a fridge and you'll never have to leave.

the wild hall

For most people the hall is a neutral space, but Wild exploits its potential for drama. Vivid colour combinations are the easiest way to tackle it. And because nothing really has to be here, extravagant concoctions can be kept here in splendid isolation. A staircase is a bonus – providing wall space on which to display favourite finds. Outlandish objects provide a *frisson* each time you pass by. It doesn't have to be a welcoming place, just stimulating.

Right Black is always a good choice for a Wild hall; it provides a visual rest without being weak or squeaky clean. The glossy walls of this hall contrast with the red room beyond. For this effect to work well, the boundaries must be clearly set, too much clutter is counterproductive. The innate extravagance of a huge bunch of flowers, especially when they are heavily scented, is both a last resort and a daily staple. Keeping an unusual light source burning all the time, such as this table uplighter, or a scented candle, evokes the drama and ambience of a Roman Catholic cathedral.

Above This hall sets the tone for what is to follow. Its shapes and colours say: vivid, original, extreme. The pair of sinuous chairs, accompanied by the surreal metallic topless palm tree make the boldest statements, and would unsettle anyone's dignity. Too much of this would be cacophony – in which case the limited space available in most halls becomes a positive asset.

the wild study

The libraries of old were worlds in themselves, where you could travel around the globe and through time without leaving the room. The Wild study is no workaday place, but somewhere to immerse yourself in knowledge and stay up all night reading if you wish. Hoard your treasures here. Colour is unimportant, but organization paramount; display everything for maximum exposure. If your CD collection is huge, consider sliding racks so that you can store twice as many; if pictures are your passion, cover walls and ceiling. Install brackets for treasured objects wherever possible – hang the dusting.

Left Shuttered and curtained windows protect the room's contents from light and ensure no risk of distraction. A large table is essential to examine volumes with ease and avoid damage, and a comfortable chair allows hours of close work. Solid shelving echoes the classical proportions: the lower cupboards continue the dado line and anchor the opulence. The ornate mirror and carpet relieve the severity, and any available light is reflected over the reader's shoulder.

Left This is a collector's paradise: pictures hung in vertical blocks give an underlying order to the principle of maximum coverage, while allowing new acquisitions to be slotted in. Even the floor is not exempt: animal skins usually given pride of place are yet another hidden pleasure. The clock concealed among the pictures provides an essential but unwelcome reminder of the world that continues to exist outside this retreat.

sensuous

Sensuous is far more of an attitude than a style, if only because sensory pleasure can be found almost anywhere, if you are looking for it. Homes dedicated entirely to feeling, rather than to doing, or seeing or having, are extremely rare. A Sensuous home is more often a (not unwelcome) by-product of the pursuit of other goals, such as opulence, truth to materials, economy or innovation.

So a house will be filled with magical amounts of sunlight and air because the designer believed these things were health-giving; a fabric can be delicious to touch because its maker was exploring ways of creating new textures. Designers of most ergonomic homes have largely ignored their Sensuous aspects. You have only to see the bleak, Bauhaus-designed, breeze-block-built terraces at Dessau-Törten, dominated by electricity pylons rather than trees, to see where the pursuit of efficiency can lead. But the urbane yet practical Eileen Gray, architect and designer, prided herself on anticipating physical desires, such as providing a sandbox in her house in the south of France in which to cool or warm the feet.

There is Sensuous pleasure to be found everywhere on the Spectrum. Minimalist John Pawson talks of the joy in contemplating the purest line. Maverick filmmaker Derek Jarman revelled in the brisk stimuli of sea salt and tar, and T. E. Lawrence took great pleasure in his ability to transcend discomfort. Visitors to Greene and Greene's ultimate Easy house have to be restrained from stroking its

expanses of smooth wood, and Wild man Jean Cocteau made it a point of honour to pursue the most esoteric physical indulgences.

But Wild's priority is sensation – to experience intense feelings, whatever they are. Sensuous wants to conserve its sensitivity to the smallest sensory input; to resensitize itself. Marcel Proust famously sequestered himself in a cork-lined boudoir to protect his senses. A striking passage in *Du côté de chez Swann* illustrates just how finely attuned they were: 'I would turn to and fro between the prayer-desk and the stamped velvet armchairs, each one always draped in its crocheted antimacassar, while the fire, baking like a pie the appetizing smells with which the room was thickly clotted, which the dewy and sunny freshness of the morning had already "raised" and started to "set", puffed them and glazed them and fluted them and swelled them into an invisible though not impalpable country cake; an immense puff-pastry, in which, barely waiting to savour the crustier, more delicate, more respectable, but also drier smells of the cupboard, the chest-of-drawers, and the patterned wall-

Left Art Nouveau designer Victor Horta created harmonious entities in which the smallest detail accorded with the whole. Obsessed with the curve, he abstracted and perfected botanical forms until his materials came alive: wooden banisters clasp hands; iron columns blossom and droop; electric lights are arranged as buds on wire stems; railings extend into the famous Horta whiplash, a large looping curve.

Above French author and notorious *bon viveur* Colette is perhaps the best source of inspiration for the Sensuous pleasures of food and domesticity. Her *Claudine* novels are full of descriptions of freshly plucked fruit. Well into old age, Colette was exercising and gourmandizing, unwilling to miss out on the fullest range of experience.

paper I always returned with an unconfessed gluttony to bury myself in the nondescript, resinous, dull, indigestible, and fruity smell of the flowered quilt.'

A home provides an interior landscape of sensory sources that can be orchestrated for maximum effect. Ilse Crawford's 1997 book *The Sensual Home* was perhaps the first interiors manual to recognize that how a home feels is as important as how it works or looks. While a sensualist will go to any lengths to satisfy their senses, the Sensuous sensibility is rather more appreciative and respectful. The Sensuous home betrays itself in many small yet telling details: arches, alcoves, textured walls; and soft brick floors, ceramic floor tiles that make you feel as if you are walking on wave-lapped sand, or a rug woven to different heights to stimulate the feet. There might be scented plants outside the bathroom window and tinkling windchimes in the hall.

Diane Ackermann, in her book *A Natural History of the Senses*, talks of how she uses sound as an emotional curtain, and vision as opium – as ways of actively blocking out the undesirable. The Sensuous sensibility is able to create just such a perfect – if unreal – world, balanced between comfort and beauty. Belgian designer Victor Horta did just that in the homes he created in Brussels at the beginning of the last century.

Horta revelled in unfamiliar domestic materials such as bare brick and cast iron, the textures and scale of which he modulated for the greatest contrast. He bathed interiors in a hyper-real light – making them as distinct as possible from leaden Belgian skies. Subtle colours unified different materials to give a sense of organic growth: writhing panels were dark at the roots and lighter towards the tip.

The ground plans of his houses freed up space, allowing it to meander and ascend through the different levels. Above all, Horta loved to play with perspective, light and shade. He used bow windows, skylights, bevelled and coloured glass, vitrified brick and large mirrors.

His own house, so outrageous at the time it was built, is shocking now only in that it is an unaccustomed sensory feast. Everywhere there is some detail to drink in and dwell on. No wonder Horta was exhausted building it: 'Why did I feel,' he wrote, 'during the course of its construction, that I had reached the summit of my happiness and that the downward curve was opening up for me?'

As the century drew on, sensory design inevitably became bolder. Gaudí's apartment block, Casa Milá, in Barcelona, remains extraordinary, with its undulating façade and intricate interlocking floorplan. The 1960s was perhaps the most physical decade yet. The fur-lined pod, in which Jane Fonda cavorts in the futuristic film *Barbarella*, is the perfect Sensuous home in miniature.

Psychedelic Danish designer Verner Panton created extraordinary forms that constantly challenged the senses, provoking new ways of seeing and living. His 'living towers' were multicoloured foam-upholstered modular seating shells, in which you could sit and lie and perch and crawl at any level.

Today's revolutionary forms remain biological in origin, but at a micro-level. Now cellular structure, rather than plant structure, excites. Whatever it is deep inside us that makes our senses respond so strongly to the abstraction of organic forms, computers and biogenetics will soon be influencing the design of some of the most sensuously satisfying homes ever.

Above Psychedelic designer Verner Panton turned furniture into spatial art. His aim was to build a coherent environment, in which carpet becomes furniture, becomes wall, becomes ceiling. In his own home, outrageous chandeliers, made up of thousands of mother-of-pearl discs suspended on chains, spread a sexy diffuse light and tinkle when moved.

Left A subtle, modern interpretation of the Oriental boudoir, with echoes of the cloistered world of the Chinese film *Raise the Red Lantern*. The lily, the flower of death, was adopted as the emblem of the Aesthetic movement, which flourished around 1900. *Fin de siècle* hedonists such as Aubrey Beardsley and Oscar Wilde loved such exotic, even sinister, imagery.

Below A ripple of sheer curtaining reminds us of what is so good about net curtains: that delicious sense of shadowy privacy and diffused light. The curvaceous lantern sculpture provides even more dappled light. Seating is simple but effective, for lounging in any configuration. The sofas form a soft boomerang, held together with the circular coffee table. The balanced curves and flow of this room evoke the aesthetic of Horta and Panton in equal measure.

the sensuous living room

Make the living room the heart of your home. Strike the right note here and the rest will follow. Think first about the room's integral qualities: How large is it? Where does the light strike in the afternoon? What atmosphere does it evoke? Then limit the range of colours, forms and textures to those that harmonize best with what the space offers. For the pleasure you take in this room to endure, you must strike a balance between comfort and beauty.

Above This is a solution that may seem extreme at first sight, but is simply a squashy sofa and a storage system taken to their logical conclusion. The paraphernalia of everyday life has been banished to the shelves, leaving the pink 'pit' as a pure pleasure zone: for watching television, chatting and drinking. It is a family place, for bouncing, rolling, snoozing and chilling out.

Left In April 1927 society decorator Syrie Maugham opened her all-white Chelsea salon to her friends at midnight. They gasped over a symphony of white, pearl, oyster and ivory enhanced with mirrors and discreet lighting. This is the single dose approach to sensual impact. The Monochrome treatment is effective in almost any colour, but white is easily the most dazzling. In this room, it is the use of texture and light within a conventional set up of comforting things – ample sofas, cushions, art, lamps, rugs, ornaments – that gives such impact.

the sensuous kitchen

The smells and textures of a living kitchen – the dense odour of baking bread, the sheen of molten jam, and the rumble of boiling potatoes – are a world in themselves. All the Sensuous kitchen has to do is allow you to enjoy these to the full. Keep your ingredients in plain view; make utensils a pleasure to handle. Windows should be large and adjustable, an outdoor seat nearby, a variety of places to stand and beat, or squat and shuck. Never ignore the impulse to perch on the table with a glass of wine and plan the next feast.

Above At first glance, this kitchen/living space may seem austere in its lines but the materials, although man-made, are utterly, deliciously Sensuous. A gleaming splashback in black glass remakes your foodstuffs as Renaissance masterpieces, while the lengthy limestone surfaces give off a soft, forgiving light. Cook in your kimono, making regular forays to recline on the shagpile and gleaming white chairs.

Below Cooking should not be an industrial process; keep it human, Italian style. Here the table used to prepare the food has been cleared, dressed and moved closer to the open air to enjoy the food. This barn-like setting has such innate atmosphere that, like the best food, it does not need much doing to it: just a few candles spaced out on the horizontal beams. If you can eat with the door to the outside world open, all the better: fresh air really does make food taste better.

the sensuous bathroom

Touch is the one sense that applies to the whole surface of the body, and so immersing the body in water is perhaps the ultimate sensory experience. A long bath reacquaints you with your own physicality. Bathing provides such unique gradations of temperature and pressure, filtering sound and light in an infinite variety of ways, that all the Sensuous bathroom has to do is to back up that experience with surfaces that echo or glisten, heavy bars of soap and soft padded mats.

Right The uninitiated would only contemplate using a luxurious sunken pool like this for a long soak in piping hot water. After a Turkish bath's regulated doses of dry and wet heat have slackened your resistance, however, entering a plunge pool such as this, filled with icy cold water, sends the sensory receptors all over your body into overdrive. You no longer register hot or cold, just an addictively intense sensation. Either way, there is nothing here to distract from total immersion in a watery world.

Right Make everything a pleasure to touch: expose your skin to extremes of texture and note the different temperatures of metal, wood, glass and tile. Remember the welcome weight of heavy towels when you are feeling giddy with heat. Here a heart-shaped nub of soap and a square of rough linen contrast with the smooth arc of the water spout. The ingenious screen of translucent squares provides privacy as well as animating the light, as it rotates unpredictably in warm air currents.

the sensuous bedroom

Left This subtle approach hints at physical pleasure in the elongated curve of the wooden chair and the generous drape of the bedspread. An old parquet floor is kind to bare feet, and the marble fire-surround and ceramic pots under the mirror provide a welcome coolness. But it is the soft, thick afternoon light that really charges the space with sensuality. Drape windows with something all enveloping and gauzy, that turns the light a creamy yellow, and ensures that the vagaries of the outside world will leave you alone.

What makes a luxurious hotel bedroom so exciting is the way the unaccustomed scale and quality of the materials stimulate bare skin: the deep pile carpet or the smoothest lacquered wood; weighty woollen blankets and voluminous feather pillows; the angle of the light though thick shades and above all, the brand-new scent of it all. To keep your own bedroom stimulating, choose satisfying basics: well-polished wood for beds and chairs, stone or wool for floors. Then rotate bedding and scents, alternate fire and flowers.

Right Panelling always creates an atmosphere of intimacy, and stripping it back to the bare pine makes it look even more relaxed. These bedclothes in linen, wool and silk, combine four different colours, but it would be hard to tire of their subtly harmonizing and contrasting lines. Although this is a large room, the same treatment, subtle yet varied, would be equally effective in a smaller space. A semi-secret cupboard, like this one in the panelling, will always stimulate the imagination.

Right A huge, dark, double-height room, that could easily have been gloomy and forbidding, has been coaxed into providing a quietly seductive place. Light muslin drapes frame and practically enclose a bed set in the centre, making the most of the physical freedom that the space provides. The fabric and the bed's fine iron frame give the room a lightness and prevent the bed overpowering the rest of the furniture. An ochre wash on the walls warms even the darkest corners, and the overlapping rugs break up the floor space and add subtle interest.

Below This hallway draws on the Japanese system of delineating rooms with screens. What would have been a blank, open space has been marked out as a harmonious whole. The repetition of simple geometric forms in soft, rich tones is soothing, while the furniture is gently curved. The geometry has a softness: the lines of the wall panels are not repeated exactly in those on the floor – this is a relaxed sense of order; far from puritanical.

the sensuous hall

It can be hard to create a Sensuous atmosphere in such a transitional space. Try to slow movement down here, to provide a place of stasis that balances the moods in other rooms. This can be achieved by breaking the space down with blocks of colour and grouping furniture, then using pools of light or scent to arrest movement. First try stopping in unaccustomed places, to see where the vista, light and ambience are most interesting.

Right Make use of interesting nooks and crannies, especially those that provide a new perspective, such as this window seat built on an unused landing. It's nothing elaborate, the heaps of white cushions are almost invisible against the white tongue and groove panelling, but it's a long way from being utilitarian. In fact, it is a completely unnecessary piece of refurbishment, but will give a disproportionate amount of pleasure. Anything that encourages you to linger in a place with no purpose is to be encouraged.

easy

The Easy sensibility is the legacy of the twentieth century. Previously, the only qualification for 'good taste' was the display of wealth and respectability, but over the past hundred years or so, other agendas have been adopted: health and efficiency; decent housing for the poor; beauty and craftsmanship in even the humblest goods. Easy homes reflect the belief that everyday living can be a perfectible process.

Its development can be traced from the early days of the Arts and Crafts movement, through 1950s Scandinavian design, to today's eco-houses. It grew out of a Christian belief in the home as a sanctuary – a heaven in miniature. The writings of British idealists William Morris and John Ruskin were highly influential. 'Why can we not have simple and beautiful dwellings fit for cultivated, well-mannered men and women?' asked Morris in 1883. 'This is the true nature of home,' asserted Ruskin, 'it is the place of Peace, the shelter, not only from all injury, but from all terror, doubt and division.'

Easy is a deeply reassuring and non-confrontational approach. It celebrates wholesome comforts, simplicity of style, and links with nature. It finds beauty not in the exquisite, novel, rare or costly, but in what is natural, apt, humble and well crafted. The Easy home is built on a human scale, comfort is paramount, everything is well balanced, neither too big nor too small.

The Easy sensibility pays great attention to details, things that ease the flow of everyday life. It provides nooks for reading and quiet activity; fixtures such as door handles are practical and pleasant to touch. By providing some sort of hearth, it acknowledges how the human impulse to gather around a source of warmth is tied into our sense of home. American architect Frank Lloyd Wright expressed this by building his homes around huge, welcoming, atavistic hearths when his contemporaries were worshipping the stealthy new gods of gas and electricity.

Easy is concerned with ergonomics and appearance, so work areas should be rationalized, but they must not be heartless. And Easy is resolutely anti-artifice. Above all, the Easy home should accommodate whatever life throws at it: children, dogs, weather, parties, sleepovers, baking sessions, carnival costume making...

Perhaps the most influential Easy home of all was the house built in 1908 by young architects and craftsmen Charles Sumner Greene and Henry Mather Greene for David Gamble in Pasadena, California, which is an Arts and Crafts masterpiece. The Greenes' aim was 'to make the whole as direct and simple as possible, but always with the

Above Charles and Ray Eames divided the double-height interior of their house into cosy and communal areas, and filled it with variegated textiles and curious souvenirs from around the world. Sliding panels allowed the sleeping areas to be reconfigured according to need.

Right Swedish artist Carl Larsson slept alone in this curtained bed, while his wife Karin lay with their children in the adjoining room. The Larsson style combined elements from folk, Viking and Japanese art, Gustavian elegance and an avant-garde emphasis on the importance of light and air.

beautiful in mind as the final goal'. The house was to be the opposite of pretension or conspicuous consumption. For them, beauty consisted not of classical allusion or abstract purity, but was rooted in nature.

The house was positioned so as to benefit from every breath of breeze, beam of light and patch of shade. Its exterior was heavily beamed and shingled, the interior 'a symphony in wood', handcrafted and polished, with tapered beams and pegged joints. The Greenes' craftsmanship brought flowers and trees into the house. A design on a leaded window echoes a rose bush outside. The home's sensuous qualities made it a magical world for children: the feel of the smooth, wooden balustrade; the sheen of the satinwood panelling; the first morning light shining through the leaded window in the massive teak front door.

Other archetypal Easy homes were those of the Swedish artists Carl and Karin Larsson and American designers Charles and Ray Eames. (It is interesting that these prime movers were couples with children – conveying the sense that a home should be designed around people and fit itself to the family. It is worth noting, too, that this concept of home should have northern European roots. Latin or Slavic European languages have no precise counterpart to the word home, which goes back to the Old Norse *heima*.)

Carl and Karin Larsson were part of a late nineteenth-century movement of artists, writers and social reformers that promoted an international ideal of domesticity. Their urge to preserve national traditions transformed the elements of the peasant home into a *Gesamtkunstwerk*, a unified work of art. They used their artistic skills to turn

an old plain farmhouse called Lilla Hyttnäs, at Sundborn, Sweden, into a poetic idyll.

It was elaborately designed to provide specific areas for every activity: from reading and weaving to keeping an eye on the children. Intimate watercolours made by Carl of their everyday life at Sundborn were published to huge acclaim in 1899 as *Ett hem* (*A Home*). They represented a fresh model of domestic life, informal and family centred, that soon came to usurp the dominant neo-renaissance Swedish style.

The mid-twentieth-century American designer Charles Eames, whose simple, elegant plywood chairs are now international icons for a new urban generation, built the Easiest house imaginable in Pacific Palisades, Los Angeles. He and his wife, Ray, built a steel and glass house designed for low cost and simple construction against a steep grassy bank, flanked by a row of ten mature eucalyptus trees. This was no minimalist box. Bright rectangles of colour were arranged Mondrian-style along the exterior. Economical, unpretentious and hugely welcoming in its use of space and materials, it was also a home that was allowed to evolve along with the lives and interests of its inhabitants.

The common-sense requirements of an Easy home are echoed in the practical considerations that underpin the complicated Eastern philosophy of feng shui, the art of arranging your life for health, wealth and happiness. The woods or mountains at your back and a long view to the front, water nearby and the morning sun filling bedroom and kitchen – all contribute to a sense of fastness and coherence with the natural order. And the use of natural, sustainable materials in the Easy home benefits the health of its inhabitants as well as the planet.

Above The simplicity of traditional Japanese woodworking techniques appeals to the Easy sensibility, which dedicates alcoves and niches not to gods but to making life that bit easier: somewhere to stash a book, a cup, a ball of wool, is always welcome.

Left Rough-and-ready, yet cosy, the homes of the American pioneers evolved into the all-American bungalow: now so popular that whole magazines are dedicated to its charms. Easy materials are reassuring and durable – waxed wood, brick, oilcloth – and while beautifully crafted, express their lack of pretension by being left unadorned.

the easy living room

Keep this room easy-going but still bright and welcoming. Think of the open living spaces that have been common in German and American houses for years and are appearing in Britain. If this room cannot be spacious it should at least be adaptable, so keep spare tables and chairs around for big family occasions. Most important of all is a convivial focal point – either a real hearth or a social centre marked out with chairs and rugs. Avoid overhead lighting, use uplighters or table lamps instead.

Right This is particularly low-key living, designed for cosy companionship rather than boisterous get-togethers. Colours are natural and restful – soft green tongue-and-groove panelling and upholstery in tones of cream and chocolate. But it is not precious: the panelling will take hard knocks and the rug and loose covers are easily washable. Everything is comfortable and should look even cosier with age. This is also a room that will respond to changing seasons: add more throws in winter, in summer take up the rug, change the loose covers and open the window wide.

Above A corner of an Easy living room demonstrates how keeping it simple need not mean stark. Contrast has been introduced into the bones of the room with storage in different tones and imaginative combinations. The shelving keeps books tidy and creates a cosy reading area, while the high-handled cupboards are dog- and child-proof. The rubber flooring is reminiscent of flagstones, but much warmer, and the urn-like table introduces curves and texture.

Left Although it was designed for warm climes, this cornucopia of oiled wood would work just as well in a cooler setting. There are echoes of the Raj in the veranda, ventilation louvres and the fretwork screen over the door, while its sliding panels and emphasis on natural wood evoke Frank Lloyd Wright and the American bungalow. The panels offer scope for creating smaller, more intimate dining or seating areas. While initially expensive to achieve, it has been carefully built using renewable resources, to create a living space that will not only last, but will improve with age.

the easy kitchen

Whether you're in here for some quick food therapy after a hard day's work, or if you spend most of your time cooking up a storm, the Easy kitchen should aim to be just that: easy on the eye, easy to use, easy to clean. Hard-wearing natural materials are tried-and-tested kitchen favourites, and many of them have specific food-enhancing properties: marble will cool pastry, for example, and wooden boards have an in-built antibacterial action. Ergonomics should always be the starting point: if you get your food–hob–worksurface triangle just right, everything else will follow.

Left It is a truism that a cook never, ever, has enough worksurfaces, so make sure that your dining table can do double duty as a preparation depot. These wicker chairs are light and easily moveable if you need to colonize extra space. The unvarnished and untreated wood of this solid refectory table absorbs clatter, won't taint food and can be scrubbed clean easily with hot water. And it is far more congenial to sit around than metal. The adjustable overhead lighting isolates the table as a dining area as well as providing fuss-free illumination for late-night jam-bottling sessions.

Left Hanging racks and open shelves are mere affectations in a kitchen that is just for show. But they are essential for the serious cook: the jars and implements are simply used too often ever to get dusty. This kitchen is as simple as can be: the cunning peephole handles on the doors ventilate the cupboards and avoid anything snagging on handles when cooking reaches one of those critical crescendos. A clock deserves pride of place in any busy kitchen.

Right This welcoming room houses
a kitchen, but is much more besides.
Unobtrusive plain white floor units and
wooden shelving are followed through
in the chair covers and window surround,
and so form a cohesive whole. Folding
doors open out completely to a terrace
that becomes part of the room for dining
alfresco. The plump sofa and armchair
make a deliberate statement of informality,
while rugs and curtains could be kept in
the chest for cooler seasons.

Right Bold diamond-patterned floor tiles delineate the shower and sink areas when the room is full of steam, allowing the actual division to be safely made of plate glass. Replacing the bath with a shower area saves on water, and makes the room look larger.

Above A heated towel rail above the bath provides a space-saving solution in a small bathroom, and means that you do not have to brave a slippery floor. A tiled border near the ceiling and skirting the base of the bath looks traditional and adds character; its warm ochre tones, also picked out in the bath towels, serve to soften the expanse of white tiles and shower curtain.

the easy bathroom

In Easy homes the bathroom is less a temple to beautification than a hard-working cleansing depot. No fancy finishes are required, but it must not be forbidding either. The answer is to opt for traditionally appropriate materials that can be cleaned and maintained easily, such as floor and wall tiles or glossy, painted wood. Extra mirrors create unnecessary work and can be potentially dangerous. Lighting should be gentle: use uplighters and fabric shades.

Above Tightly sealed and painted wood panelling feels warm and lived in, and hides a tangle of unsightly pipes. Continued around the sink, the panelling creates a useful storage cupboard, and allows for a shallow cubbyhole behind the mirror. The freestanding bathtub has been chosen for its curvaceous form, which contrasts with the strong verticals of the panelling, and the legs give the room space to breathe.

the easy bedroom

Whether it is a retreat from the family or open house, the Easy bedroom should signal a change of pace from the rest of the house. It is the place to keep heirlooms and treasures, and it can be a haven of more indulgent fabrics. Deal with practical constraints with aplomb: Carl Larsson set his bed in the centre of an awkwardly shaped bedroom which had more doors and windows than walls. Imagination and simplicity can provide the most striking effects.

Right Use honeyed tones in extremes of light and dark and the effect will be warming and reassuring. Here, the irregular curve of the sloping wall has been made into a cave-like feature with the use of contrasting paint. A dark area at the head of the bed indicates oblivion — a strong signal that the day begins and ends here. Plain, pale Roman blinds add visual interest without taking up as much room as curtains, and echo the stripes of the blanket. The huge wicker pot is an object of natural beauty, and can store a multitude of things without looking too formal.

Above There is much to be said for a bed that has been made traditionally with sheets and blankets. They give more seasonal flexibility and create a cleaner line than bulky duvets. Knowing how to make a bed neatly is one of the elemental acts of homemaking. The horizontal boarding of this basic bedroom evokes the homesteader lifestyle of American pioneer days.

Below Avoiding strong colours and oppressive shapes in the hall allows you a breathing space from the onslaught of activities taking place in other rooms. And while you are there, a solid banister adjacent to the airing cupboard provides a useful place to fold linen and drape items in transit between floors. Natural wood floorboards like these may look high maintenance, but with a couple of coats of varnish they will last for years and usefully reflect the light.

the easy hall

As the Easy home's central conduit, a well-used hall will buzz with the echoes of domestic life. It has to cope with heavy traffic, noise and clutter, so keep it as open and well lit as you can. Make sure it works as a voice-tunnel, allowing you to call out to the farther recesses of your home. The floor and walls should be clutter-free, easy to clean, hard-wearing and, of course, free from fragile ornament. Keep it cheery by flooding it with yellow-toned light.

Above A galleried landing does not have to be grand. This modern version, with its slatted boardwalk and a cottage-style internal window, creates a real holiday atmosphere. Combined with the bridge-like effect of the contrasting flooring, the curving lilac wall subtly conveys a sense of entering the more peaceful part of this home. Just keep the finish natural and the colours clean and warm.

urban

The Urban sensibility is elegant and sophisticated. It is rooted in the Enlightenment movement of the eighteenth century, when cities all over Europe witnessed an explosion of scientific knowledge and high culture. Ever since then, if you wanted to be somebody, the city was the place to be. To be Urban is to be forward-looking and part of the elite. Even an early Romantic such as Wordsworth, while fearful of the city's power, acknowledged its dangerous allure.

The city's chaotic mass began to be moulded by the forces of rationality into an artificial, gridded and self-referential world that rapidly put more and more distance between itself and its organic roots. And within the Georgian home too, simple, disciplined proportion was thought to provide the key to perfection. Theorists such as Robert Morris believed that the pursuit of mathematical harmony would enable the home to mirror what contemporary philosophers revered as the ideal beauty of nature. He based his universal rule of proportion for all rooms on Palladio, reducing buildings to elemental shapes: cubes, squares and circles.

The Urban mentality applies this reductionist approach to day-to-day living. If it could, Urban would start every new home from scratch, casting out the extraneous and the incidental, revelling in its own grand scheme. Having a house built to order is the ultimate Urban dream. This confers status, for sure, but more crucially provides the pure satisfaction of total aptness.

Unlike the Easy sensibility, the Urban mind is interested in the radical solution for its own sake. It is forward thinking, excited by innovation and rigour, and will sacrifice much to 'line'. The modern architectural mind instinctively approaches the world in this way, as, often, do the politician and philosopher. Urban does not like to acknowledge that life is a messy business, but if it is, then surely it can and should be contained. A good contemporary example is the laboratory-like home designed in 1998 by Ulla and Lasse Vahtera for the Laitinen family of scientists in Finland. A severe white plaster and metal box, it is a cool, sensible home, squared off into neat, balanced sections.

The Laitinen home expresses little sense of conventional luxury. But insisting on the more esoteric luxury of adopting the most sophisticated and apt solution is a key Urban attribute. This beguiling combination of sensibility and reason is embodied by the resolute, self-taught designer, Irishwoman Eileen Gray, whose work was at once

Below left, top The 6 x 14 metre living room of Eileen Gray's E-1027 is partitioned to allow maximum flexibility. Floor cushions extend the divan bed to 4 metres.

Below left, bottom Eileen Gray's bulbous Bibendum chair was never conceived as a theatrical or fashionable prop, although it has since been used as such.

Below In Mies van der Rohe's single-storey rectangular pavilion, Farnsworth House, dark wood counteracts the exposure of vast glass walls.

luxurious and stark, elegant, economical and discreet. Although she was a close associate of stringent Modernists such as Le Corbusier, over-schematic solutions were anathema to Gray's artistic training and temperament.

The lines of her early work were sober, sweeping and tapered, the effect was of fine-tuned contrast, with sensual tactile surfaces tempered by a certain austerity of line and decoration. She was utterly disdainful of the florid Art Deco and Louis-something styles she saw around her: 'Lots of it makes me feel quite sick,' she later said. For her first big exhibition in 1923 she produced a black lacquer divan bed, a large red and matt-white screen, a dark blue and brown carpet and various hanging lights, austere and rigorous in effect, despite the richness of the materials.

As she became more interested in architectural schemes and the use of technology for mass production, she applied her discrimination to the processes of living. Soon she was designing all the fittings of life, either as folding, moving pieces, or as integral features of the architecture. A capacious dressing cabinet with asymmetrical doors and cork-fronted pivoting drawers also functioned as a room divider and dressing screen. She produced a tubular steel table which extended like a trombone – the circular bedside version with a built-in handle is now a design classic.

By 1927 Gray had built her own perfect house, which she called, tersely, E-1027. A small, isolated holiday home near Monte Carlo in the south of France, designed with Romanian architect Jean Badovici, it was a tardis-like space that opened out in infinite variations. She went to town on the detailing: hinged flaps, swivel trays, flip-flop

top folding tables on wheels, witty rugs with maritime allusions... Gray was excited by intricate mechanisms, complex and ingenious arrangements that reused supposedly industrial materials in lavish, powerful ways.

An element of connoisseurship remains a key Urban attribute even when it is disguised as stealth wealth. An early example was Cedric Gibbons and Dolores del Rio's house, built in 1930 in Santa Monica. It is full of terrazzo, gunite (smart stucco), copper sheeting painted celadon green, and quarter-inch-thick, high-tech battleship linoleum in jet black. The dominant colours are ivory and soft lemon, the fabrics silk and velour. The bathroom, in titillating black marble, has screw-heads on mirrors shaped like stars.

Another example, the Art Deco treasure Eltham Palace in London, verges on the kitsch, but the eagerness of its 1930s owners Virginia and Stephen Courtauld to embrace new technology is pure Urban. A payphone in the foyer allowed guests to make (then very expensive) phone calls, loudspeakers broadcast music throughout the ground floor, there was a built-in vacuum cleaning system, and even the pet lemur's quarters were centrally heated. But simple touches, such as positioning Virginia's washbasin so that her passionately loved garden was the first thing she saw every day, would also have appealed to Eileen Gray.

Today, our homes are absorbing wave upon wave of new technology, and we no longer have to live in the city to be of the city. The Urban sensibility embraces all this, but finds a way to fine-tune its effects. The flatscreen television, fibre optics and the descendants of wireless application protocol will make those of an Urban disposition happy indeed.

Above While it pushes the boundaries of what Gray would consider good taste, styles such as the rather more flamboyant West Coast Art Moderne appeal to the Urban sensibility for its sheer luxurious attention to detail.

Left Urban sees the home not as a cellular structure that fulfils a nesting instinct, but as the intersection of various planes of reality. Each plane functions as a place to eat, sleep, bathe and socialize, and the goal is to give each of these planes its perfect expression in form.

the urban living room

This room is the interface between your public and private lives, so make sure it satisfies both. The Urban sensibility is organized, maintaining distinct arenas for different activities, and consistent in taste, ensuring each area flows smoothly into the next. Create a neutral shell, with large, well-finished surfaces and unobtrusive colours, to fix the focus on your furnishings. Invest in the very best you can afford, right down to electric sockets and switches.

Above Exercising constant restraint can produce the most elegant results, as long as everything is well finished. Echo small details such as the wide border seen here on the rug and the picture frames, to hold the room together. Balance angular items such as this table and the sofa with the more subtle curves of the Eames chair and the baby grand piano. Setting large paintings on custom-built shelves is at once informal and extravagant. The limited palette maintains a measured mood.

Below This is large-scale urban living with real impact. The room's true expanse reveals itself as the visitor emerges from a staircase placed dramatically at its centre. The stairwell serves to mark out the use of space, from the kitchen area on the rear left, to the dining area by the windows, to the seating area in the foreground. Large pieces of furniture built with clean, flowing lines are given enough breathing space to make bold individual statements. The sheer bulk of the solid wooden seating is hugely impressive. Such pieces can be specially commissioned or salvaged. This, for example, may have come from the hall of a now-deserted railway station.

Below The dado rail functioned originally to prevent chair backs from damaging expensive wall finishes. Here, a similarly elegant effect has been achieved, to equally practical purpose. At the point at which the hearthstone runs into a low shelf, the adjacent surfaces have been linked with storage lockers beneath. Centring the single ornament and picture in an alcove gives them added gravitas, while keeping the line of the furniture (and most of the visual interest) at such a low level serves to emphasize the height of the room.

Right Using colour in large but subtle blocks avoids the need for extraneous detail. The generous dimensions and clean lines of this seating configuration provide ample room without visual clutter. The shadow-gap skirting detail, the hole in the coffee table, and the furniture's slim tubular legs all seem to enlarge the floor space and prevent the large blocks of colour on the wall, and in the seating, from sitting too heavily on the floor. These semi-industrial, neutral-toned Crittall windows never look less than sleek since they never need painting.

the urban kitchen

It is important to strike a balance between the functional and the elegant: while truly industrial kitchens are full of clutter, over-refined kitchens crack as easily as eggs when faced with the smallest culinary task. Ever since Margarete Schütte-Lihotzky built the world's first fitted kitchen in Frankfurt in 1927 – all concrete sinks and built-in storage – the kitchen has moved from being the subterranean realm of hard toil to the acknowledged heart of the Urban home, worthy of the most sophisticated and streamlined furniture.

Below A modish circular table works here to counteract the hard surfaces and looming bulk of the steel fridge. The cabinet is the epitome of pared-down, unobtrusive design: its sliding doors present a clean surface and it is fixed at an unobtrusive and easy-to-reach height.

Left This kitchen is definitely at the industrial end of the scale. It has all the modern vernacular elements: glass bricks, stainless-steel worksurfaces, exposed air vent, looped halogen lights and hooked hanging racks. But, marooned here in splendid isolation on a pale laminated floor, it has a coherent charm. Using industrial elements in parentheses like this is only effective if the finish is perfect.

the urban bathroom

There should be no hint of the prosaic here. The Urban bathroom is
an aspirational dream of serviced hotel luxury. Le Corbusier decreed
that a bathroom be designed on the scale of a drawing room, and
supplied with every ablutionary accessory. But since most bathrooms
are still relatively small, even minor extravagances here have major
impact. Large mirrors are too unsubtle: use unusual materials instead,
and isolate each piece of sanitaryware for iconic impact.

Above Philippe Starck's monumental, tapered
cylindrical forms are archetypes of the Urban
bathroom. This is ergonomics as sculpture.
A space-saving device, such as running the
towel rail around the rim of the bath, has
both practical and aesthetic merit. And the
general warmth of the colour scheme keeps
the room opulent rather than clinical.

Above Replacing the everyday details with the unexpected, such as these shaped wooden joists on which the bath rests like a boat in dock, keep the eye stimulated in what could be an overly clean space. The generous glass shelf is impressive, and the highly varnished wall ensures a play of light and shadow.

Left For the Urban sensibility, the high-maintenance bathroom is as much of a trophy as the high-maintenance wife. This custom-made stainless-steel bath will require regular polishing if it is not to look like an industrial mixing bowl – but ingenious touches, such as the aluminium screen and fibre-optic lights will turn daily ablutions into daily drama.

the urban study

A sleek and efficient home workplace is very important to the Urban sensibility, which reveres intellectual curiosity and technological know-how. The study should be totally integrated into the home, and its design should be equally as sophisticated as that of the general living areas. The Urban study uses Continental intellectual traditions as a reference, with the inclusion of custom-built, high-quality shelves and desks, and incorporating art and sculpture as a given. Anticipate this need in your design, and edit any more mundane clutter regularly.

Below Set close to an open window where the sounds of the street are a constant reminder of city life, this simple work area is less a retreat than a staging post in a busy life. The art dominates, the arrangement is gratifyingly measured. The brown banding of the picture frames and desk lamp, and the upholstered armchair, ground what could have been an unsettling and transient space.

Left The matching ladder, with its sturdy handrails, enables this soaring library arrangement to make full use of the height of this room. The armchair and footstool suggest an updated version of the country-house library, but any lingering association with dustiness or gloom is shrugged off in a spacious, clean setting that exudes confidence and vigour. Designing extra-deep shelves allows books to be ranked in double rows if necessary. Do more exquisite and large-format books justice by including some double-height shelving too.

the urban bedroom

There is nothing kitsch about the Urban sensibility, although it does have a dry wit. Consequently the bedroom, which so often displays the flip side of an outwardly cool persona, has nothing to hide. If anything, the Urban bedroom must be less wearing on the eye than any other room. Its colour and forms should provide reassurance and solid comfort. Dark, sombre tones and minimal detailing are the visual equivalent of one last brandy before bedtime.

Above Heavily curtained and shuttered, this is the bedroom to have when life is moving too fast and intensive rest is required. The tailor's dummy, the cabinet and the stack of trunks provide restrained visual interest and introduce paler tones; they might also have a practical use when disrobing. The crisp, turned-down sheets and pinstriped blanket will encourage an ordered and businesslike state of mind on waking.

Below Far from being a claustrophobic cell, this expansive yet rigorous bedroom ensures that the sleeper will shed the cares of the day. Setting the bed in the centre of the room makes a nightly ritual out of turning in. An opaque glass door and wardrobe distance the sleeper from clothes and the outside world, turning them instead into a wall of shadowy shapes. The purpose of the twin cylinders at the head of the bed is obscure, but they strike a suitable balance between the classical and the industrial.

Above This stairwell cuts through the home and provides a central sculptural element. Careful lighting suggests hidden depths. The lines are stark, but it is not so purist as to forget about providing a sturdy handrail, or deny that horizontal surfaces are good stacking places, especially for items in transit around the house. Such a dominating feature could overwhelm if it were not treated sensitively in colour and finish.

the urban hall

The hall is the barometer of the Urban home, providing visitors' first impressions and functioning as an important circulating area during parties. It offers a sense of the home beyond, and a place to display art, and from which to glance into other rooms. Good, flexible lighting is crucial to regulate mood and atmosphere. None of the clutter of everyday life should be on display: no bicycles or vacuum cleaners – unless these are works of art in their own right.

Left A full-length skylight is mirrored in the reinforced glass floor of this impressive hallway. Flanked with colourful art, a corridor that could have been dull and depressing is now an aesthetic experience. If you do not have access to natural light, an illuminated false ceiling can give a similar effect.

Above This corridor uses the same tricks as the main picture (left): transparent roofing, and a bold focal point that appears to foreshorten the vista. But glazed doors have divided its length into zones and ensure an awareness of spaces beyond. This sort of unobtrusive flexibility is always useful.

index

acknowledgements

Bibliography

Authentic Decor by Peter Thornton, Weidenfeld & Nicholson, UK 1993

Colour by Paul Zelanski and Mary Pat Fisher, Herbert Press, London 1989

Colour Art and Science edited by Trevor and and Janine Bourriau, Cambridge University Press, UK 1995

From Bauhaus to Our House by Tom Wolfe, Abacus, UK 1983

Geography of Home by Akiko Busch, Princeton Architectural Press, NY 1999

Home: The Twentieth Century House by Deyan Sudjic, Lawrence King 1999

House as a Mirror of Self by Clare Cooper Marcus, Conari Press, California 1997

If this House Could Talk by Elizabeth Smith Brownstein, Simon & Schuster, NY1999

Pioneers of Modern Design by Nikolaus Pevsner, Penguin, London 1988

The Beginner's Guide to Colour Psychology by Angela Wright, Kyle Cathie, UK1988

The Poetics of Space by Gaston Bachelard, Beacon Press, Boston 1994

The Power of Place by Winifred Gallagher, Harper Perennial 1993

Writers' Houses by Francesca Premoli-Droulers, Cassell, UK 1995

Acknowledgements

The publisher thanks the following photographers and organizations for their kind permission to reproduce the photographs in this book:

2 left Gilles de Chabaneix/Marie Claire Maison (sty: Marie Kalt); 2 centre Andrew Bordwin 2 right Maura McEvoy;3 left Brian Harrison/Red Cover; 3 centre Marie Pierre Morel/Marie Claire Maison (sty: Christine Puech); 3 right Simon Upton (des: Dolce & Gabbana)/The Interior Archive; 4–5 Dennis Gilbert/ View (arch: Rich Mather); 6 above Edina van der Wyck/The Interior Archive (arch: Josh Schweitzer); 6 below Ray Main/Mainstream; 9 above Ray Main/Mainstream (arch: Phillip Meadowcroft/ James Birch); 9 below Edina van der Wyck/The Interior Archive; 14 left Mads Mogensen; 14 centre Joe Cornish; 14 right Chris Chapman Photography; 15 left Joe Cornish/Arcaid; 15 centre Joe Beynon/Axiom Photographic Agency; 15 right Henry Bourne (arch: Jo Crepain); 16 above E. Bjurstrom/Middle East Pictures; 16 below Tony Waltham/Robert Harding Picture Library; 17 above Alaine Evrard/Impact; 17 above centre Chris Coe/Axiom Photographic Agency; 17 below centre Richard Bryant/Arcaid (arch: Gabriel Poole); 17 below Heather Angel; 18 above Michel Arnaud/Inside/The Interior Archive; 18 below Bill Batten/World of Interiors;19 above Andrew Wood/Interior Archive; 19 above centre Antonio Martinelli; 19 below centre Michael Freeman; 19 below Jacques Dirand/World of Interiors; 20 left Jan Verlinde (des: Jan Wals); 20 centre Tim Young/Living etc/ipc Syndication; 20 right James Morris/ Axiom Photographic Agency; 21 left Pacal Chevalier/World of Interiors; 21 centre Richard Waite; 21 right Marc Broussard & Catherine Taralon; 22 above James Morris/Axiom Photographic Agency (arch: John Pawson); 22 above centre Ray Main/Mainstream; 22 below Paul Ryan/International Interiors (des: Sharone Einhorn); 23 above G. Howard/Camera Press; 23 centre Ray Main/Mainstream; 23 below Christian Sarramon;24 left Monkwell (design: Honeywell Moss); 24 centre Maia Diver Fabrics (design: Olivia); 24 right G.P. & J. Baker (design: Graphite K0316); 25 left Monkwell (design: Berber Non Fr Tribal); 25 centre Bentley & Spiers (design: Conelli); 25 right The Gainsborough Silk Weaving Co. Ltd.(design: F1912); 26 Artisan; 27 above & centre Artisan; 27 Integra Products; 28 left Christie's Images (des: Mies Van Der Rohe, 1929); 28 centre Christie's Images (des: Julius Jirasek, 1935/7); 28 right Christie's Images (des: William Morris, 1856, painted by Rossetti); 29 left Christie's Images (physics by Michele Oka Doner, 1990); 29 centre Christie's Images (des: Gerald Summers, 1933-4); 29 right Christie's Images (des: Rolf Sachs, 1994); 30 above Luke White/Axiom Photographic Agency; 30 centre Guy Obijn; 30 below Andrew Wood/ The Interior Archive (des: Jo Malone); 31 above James Merrell/World of Interiors; 31 centre Edina van der Wyck/The Interior Archive; 31 below Andrew Bordwin (arch: Bill Sofield); 33 Verner Panton Design; 34 Sigrid Geske/Stiftung Weimarer Klassik; 38 above Verne Fotografie (arch: Nathalie van Reeth); 38 centre Alexander van Berge; 38 below Alexandre Bailhache/Marie Claire Maison (sty: Marie Guibert); 40 Marie Pierre Morel /Marie Claire Maison (sty: C. Puech/ M. Kalt); 41 left Ray Main/Mainstream (des: Roger Oates); 41 right Antoine Bootz /Marie Claire Maison (sty: Catherine Ardouin); 43 above Joe Beynon/Axiom Photographic Agency; 43 above centre James Morris /Axiom Photographic Agency (arch: John Pawson); 43 below Alexandre Bailhache /Marie Claire Maison (sty: Marie Guibert); 46 above Verne Fotografie; 46 centre Verne Fotografie; 46 below Jacques Dirand/The Interior Archive; 47 above Simon Upton/The Interior Archive; 47 centre Jan Verlinde (arch: Nathalie Van Reeth); 47 below Verne Fotografie; 50 above Dennis Gilbert/The National Trust Photographic Library; 50 below Gilles des Chabaneix /Marie Claire Maison (sty: Catherine Ardouin); 51 Dennis Gilbert/The National Trust Photographic Library; 52–3 Chris Gascoigne/View (arch: Stanton Williams); 53 above Andrew Wood/The Interior Archive; 53 below Cindy Palmano (arch: John Pawson); 54 Eric Morin (des: Christine Baillou); 54-5 Jan Verlinde (arch: Lowette); 56 Andrew Bordwin; 57 Jan Verlinde (arch: John Pawson for Obumex); 58 Paul Ryan/International Interiors (des: Kastrup & Sjunnesson); 59 Verne Fotografie (arch: Carlos Zapata); 60–1 Jacques Caillaut; 61 right Simon Upton/The Interior Archive (des: Anthony Collett); 62 Richard Davies; 63 Verne Fotografie (des: Glenn Sestig); 64–5 A.F. Pelissier/Maison Madame Figaro; 66 Don Freeman/World of Interiors; 67 Verne Fotografie (Claire Bataille & Paul Ibens for Obumex); 68 Howard Sooley; 69 The Charlston Trust; 70–1 Ricardo Labougle (des: Juan Ricci); 72 left Fernando Bengoechea/The Interior Archive; 72–3 Nicolas Tosi /Marie Claire Maison (sty: Catherine Ardouin); 74 Gross and Daley; 75 Jim Goldberg; 76–7 Mirjam Bleeker & Frank Visser/Taverne Agency; 77 right Don Freeman/World of Interiors; 78 Marc Broussard & Catherine Taralon; 79 Andreas von Einsiedel /Red Cover (des: Frederic Mechiche); 80 Marc Broussard & Catherine Taralon (bedspread by J.F. Lesage); 81 Don Freeman/World of Interiors;82 Simon Upton/The Interior Archive (des: Anthony Collett); 83 Marie Pierre Morel /Marie Claire Maison (sty: Christine Puech); 84–5 Pascal Chevalier/ World of Interiors; 85 right Andrew Wood/The Interior Archive; 86–7 courtesy Hearst San Simeon State Historical Monument; 88 Hulton-Deutsch Collection/Corbis; 89 Jen Fong photography (Tsao & Mcknown Architects); 90 Simon Upton (des: Carol Thomas)/The Interior Archive; 91 Simon Upton/The Interior Archive (des: Dolce & Gabbana); 92–3 Greg Delves/Judy Casey Inc.; 94 left Rene Stoeltie; 94–5 Fritz von Schulenberg/The Interior Archive (des: Nicholas Haslam); 96 Christoph Dugied/Marie Claire Maison (sty: Josee Postic); 97 Rene Stoeltie; 98 Greg Delves/Judy Casey Inc.; 99 Sari Visi/Camera Press; 100 Verne Fotografie (designer: Glenn Sestig); 101 Verne Fotografie; 102 Simon Upton/World of Interiors; 103 Laura Resen/Lachapelle Representation; 104–5 Richard Bryant/Arcaid; 105 right Pierre Hussenot/Agence Top; 106–7 Richard Bryant/Arcaid (Tsao & Mckown Architects); 107 right Verner Panton Design; 108–9 Jen Fong photography (Tsao & Mckown Architects); 109 right Richard Davies; 110 Winfried Heinze/Living etc/ipc Syndication; 112 left Trevor Mein; 112–13 Marc Broussard & Catherine Taralon; 114 Nicolas Tosi /Marie Claire Maison (sty: Postic/Renault); 115 Marie Pierre Morel/ Marie Claire Maison;116 Gilles de Chabaneix /Marie Claire Maison(sty: Marie Kalt); 117 David George/ Homes & Gardens/ipc Syndication; 118–9 Antonio Maniscalco; 120–1 Mathew Donaldson/ World of Interiors/Condé Nast Publications; 121 right Hotze Eisma (sty: Rianne Laydstra); 122 Julius Shulman (arch: Charles & Ray Eames); 123 Carl Larsson–garden; 124–5 Laurent Teisseire /Marie Claire Maison (sty: Catherine Ardouin); 125 right Marianne Majerus; 126 Reiner Blunck (arch: Mark Mack); 127 T. Stewart/Living etc/ipc Syndication; 128–9 Reiner Blunck (arch: John Mainwaring); 130 left Alexander van Berge; 130–1 Hilary Jeanne/ Marie Claire Maison (sty: Catherine Ardouin); 132–3 David Brittain/ Domain; 134–5 Alexander van Berge; 135 right Brian Harrison/Red Cover; 136 Debi Treloar/Red Magazine/ Emap Elan; 137 Mads Mogensen; 138–9 Alexander van Berge; 139 right Julie Phipps/Arcaid (arch: Cowper Griffith Associates); 140 above & below Philippe Garner (des: Eileen Gray); 141 Peter Cook (arch: Mies Van Der Rohe)/View; 142–3 Verne Fotografie (arch: Johan Laethem); 143 right Hotze Eisma (sty: Rianne Laydstra); 144 left Verne Fotografie (des: Didier Gomez); 144–5 Jan Verlinde (arch: Lowette); 146 left Verity Welstead/Narratives; 146–7 Antoine Bootz/Marie Claire Maison (sty: Catherine Ardouin); 148 Simon Upton/The Interior Archive; 149 Guy Obijn; 150 left Guy Obijn; 150–1 James Merrell /Elle Decoration (Brookes Stacey Architects); 151 right Ray Main/Mainstream; 152 Verne Fotografie; 153 Verne Fotografie (des: Didier Gomez); 154 left Brian Harrison (des: Nicholas Haslam)/Red Cover; 154–5 Guy Obijn; 156 left Hotze Eisma (sty: Rianne Laydstra); 156–7 Guy Obijn.